Praise for *God's Story in 66 Verses*

"The old, old story of the gospel is root[...]
which is the theme of the whole Bible. W[...]
and moving fast, Stan Guthrie shows h[...]
to both stories. Excellent!"

— J. I. Packer, Board of Governors'
Professor of Theology at Regent
College

"Thomas Cranmer once said that the Bible was meant to be read, marked, learned, and inwardly digested. This book is a spiritual digestive for an up-close and personal encounter with God's Word—key verses from each of the canonical books. A great resource for devotion and prayer."

— Timothy George, founding dean of
Beeson Divinity School at Samford
University and general editor of the
Reformation Commentary on Scripture

"Stan Guthrie provides a much-needed tonic to our sleepy, biblically illiterate culture. This book will help many people move beyond the shallow, simple-minded myths of what the Bible is about, to actually grasp its grand narrative. And it does it one verse at a time. Buy it, give it away—and don't forget to read it yourself."

— Josh Moody, senior pastor of College
Church in Wheaton, Illinois

"So often we read little bits of the Bible with little sense of how they fit into the larger book and therefore we miss the real point. In *God's Story in 66 Verses*, Stan Guthrie presents little bits of the Bible that actually lead us to the real point of each book of the Bible. This will be a great help to those who are new to the Bible as well as to those of us who've been reading the Bible a long time and tend to ignore the parts we just don't get."

— Nancy Guthrie, author of the Seeing
Jesus in the Old Testament Bible
study series

"The Bible is a book so deep no mortal will ever get to the bottom of it. Nevertheless, because God has revealed His wisdom to us, all benefit by seeking to understand the Scriptures as best they can. Though we never get the last word about the Bible, it is possible to have a sure word. Stan Guthrie has produced a book that gets to the 'sure word,' and makes it accessible to all. His approach is relatively simple: find the central verse of each book of the Bible that clarifies the theme of that book. For those who want to go deeper, begin with *God's Story in 66 Verses*."

— Jerry Root, PhD, associate professor
at Wheaton College and visiting
professor at Biola University

"This helpful book can overcome our tendency to, as Francis Schaeffer put it, 'see the world in bits and pieces.' In the Bible, we find the truest story there is of all things and all of us. And Stan Guthrie lays it out carefully and creatively."

— John Stonestreet, speaker and fellow,
the Chuck Colson Center for Christian
Worldview; senior content advisor,
Summit Ministries

"With his characteristic clarity and depth, Stan Guthrie highlights God's story from all of Scripture, serving a delectable feast of biblical truth. If you are hungry for God's Word, look no further."

— Chris Castaldo, director of the
Ministry of Gospel Renewal,
Wheaton College

"Stan Guthrie combines a clever approach to remembering the biblical books collectively with a concise approach to the books individually. His clarity and brevity are refreshing and readable."

— Jerry Pattengale, assistant provost,
Indiana Wesleyan University and
executive director of Green Scholars
Initiative

"I never miss a Stan Guthrie book. I consider him one of the most refreshing and cogent Evangelical thinkers writing today."

— Jerry B. Jenkins, owner of the Christian Writers Guild

"We face an epidemic of biblical illiteracy in our culture. Most Americans—especially those in the younger generation—have scant engagement with Scripture. And getting them to read the Bible is no easy task. It's a big book! For a generation that doesn't know Paul from Potiphar, it can be daunting just to crack the cover. That's why I'm excited about *God's Story in 66 Verses*. Guthrie has created a brilliant way to introduce readers to the broad themes of Scripture. With crisp prose and a disarming tone, Guthrie distills the biblical witness while showing how all of Scripture points to Christ. I pray many people will read this important book and come to know the Scriptures and the God whom they reveal."

— Drew Dyck, managing editor of *Leadership Journal* and author of *Yawning at Tigers: You Can't Tame God, So Stop Trying*

"What a great idea for a book, and how skillfully executed! *God's Story in 66 Verses* will help make the Bible accessible and compelling for a distracted generation perpetually on the move."

— Louis Markos, professor of English and Scholar-on-Residence, Houston Baptist University

"The most common mistake in reading the Bible—whether by laypeople or theologians—is to emphasize certain texts in a way that conflicts with the whole arc of Scripture. Stan Guthrie's new book provides a superb corrective to that tendency, to which all of us are vulnerable at times."

— John Wilson, editor of *Books & Culture*

GOD'S STORY

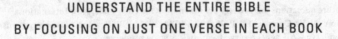

UNDERSTAND THE ENTIRE BIBLE
BY FOCUSING ON JUST ONE VERSE IN EACH BOOK

STAN GUTHRIE

NELSON
BOOKS

An Imprint of Thomas Nelson

Published in Nashville, Tennessee, by Nelson Books, an imprint of Thomas Nelson. Nelson Books and Thomas Nelson are registered trademarks of HarperCollins Christian Publishing, Inc.

Thomas Nelson titles may be purchased in bulk for educational, business, fund-raising, or sales promotional use. For information, please e-mail SpecialMarkets@ThomasNelson.com.

Some material on the book of Psalms was adapted from the *Baker Encyclopedia of the Bible*, 1988, edited by Walter A. Elwell, Baker Academic, a division of Baker Publishing Group. Used by permission.

Unless otherwise noted, Scripture quotations are taken from the English Standard Version. © 2001 by Crossway Bibles, a division of Good News Publishers.

Scripture quotations marked NIV are taken from the Holy Bible, New International Version®, NIV®. Copyright © 1973, 1978, 1984, 2011 by Biblica, Inc.™ Used by permission of Zondervan. All rights reserved worldwide. www.zondervan.com

Library of Congress Cataloging-in-Publication Data

Guthrie, Stan.
  God's story in 66 verses : understand the entire Bible by focusing on just one verse in each book / Stan Guthrie.
     pages cm
  Includes bibliographical references.
  ISBN 978-1-4002-0642-1
  1. Bible—Introductions. I. Title. II. Title: God's story in sixty-six verses.
  BS475.3.G88 2015
  220.6'1—dc23   2014005812

Printed in the United States of America

15 16 17 18 19 RRD 6 5 4 3 2 1

To John Wilson . . . friend, colleague, encourager

Contents

NEW TESTAMENT

Introduction

HOW DO YOU, AS THE OLD SAYING GOES, EAT AN ELEPHANT? *ONE bite at a time*. How do you digest the Bible? *One verse at a time*. The Bible can be a difficult book for the average person to understand. Written over the span of a millennium and a half, and completed nearly two thousand years ago, the Book of books sometimes seems like a mishmash of stories and literary styles. We can get so caught up in the Bible's details that we lose sight of its big picture.

It's easy to see the thirty-nine books of the Old Testament and the twenty-seven books of the New Testament as simply a collection of familiar narratives—the Flood covering the earth, the Israelites going through the Red Sea on dry land, Lazarus being raised—and characters such as Adam and Eve, Moses, and the apostle Paul. For many people, Scripture is a confusing collection of ancient literature without a coherent theme. And indeed, with nearly twelve hundred chapters in a dizzying array of literary genres—poetry, history, parable, and so on—the Bible can seem like a big and intimidating book.

So how are we to get a handle on Scripture as a whole and on these sixty-six unique books without becoming Bible scholars? This book, *God's Story in 66 Verses*, is my answer. It will offer you quick, lay-level access into Scripture via one *key verse* for each of the Bible's books, from Genesis to Revelation. You might ask, "Why just *one* verse per Bible book when there are more than thirty-one thousand verses in the Old and New Testaments, and why these *particular* verses?"

Good questions! I'm the first to admit that there is nothing magical about examining one verse for every book. Let's be honest—the chapter and verse divisions we have in our Bibles today are not sacred—though, in the providence of God, they have proved to be enormously helpful. Can you imagine trying to find something in your Bible without them?

The first Bibles—in Hebrew, Aramaic, and Greek—were written on scrolls and had no chapters and verses. The first English Bible to use verse numbering as we have it today was the Geneva Bible in 1560. (The venerable King James Bible came along in 1611.) Our chapters and verses are merely a human-created convenience to help us navigate the text—an extremely important one. But I am convinced that each Bible book has at least one verse that summarizes or lays the foundation for that book, placing it in context with the rest of God's Word (which, in total, is one unified, variegated message to mankind for our good and his glory). They will give you insight into Scripture in ways that traditional approaches often don't.

And please note: the key verses you will encounter in this volume have not been chosen because they are what I consider "the best" or are among my personal favorites (though some are). They are highlighted because I believe they most accurately represent the books in which they reside and Scripture as a whole.

For example, although you might suspect that the key verse for Genesis would be chapter 1, verse 1, "In the beginning, God created the heavens and the earth," I have chosen 15:6, "[Abram] believed the LORD, and he counted it to him as righteousness." That's because the verse illustrates how the covenant-keeping Lord (the Creator of all) saves his people *through faith*—in Genesis as well as in both Testaments.

In addition to presenting the key verses, this volume provides a brief commentary on every Bible book. God has given each Bible book to his people for good reason, and this volume will help you get something out of each one. As you read through, absorb, and refer to this volume, you will learn how the key verses (and the books they represent) fit together in a unified message, what the main thrust of Scripture is, and what difference it should make in your daily life.

Rather than sift and sort through all thirty-one thousand verses to figure out what the Bible is all about, you will learn it through the sixty-six key verses quickly, easily, and painlessly. (I will sometimes set them off in italics so that you will be able to find them more easily when they are presented as part of a larger passage.) When you open these windows into God's Word, understanding the Bible will no longer be a mystery.

In the back, you'll also find a separate listing of the sixty-six verses, helping you memorize or share them with others. You'll see the volumes I used to help me understand the Bible's sixty-six books—most especially the ultrahelpful *ESV Study Bible* (which combines my favorite translation with extensive notes, articles, outlines, charts, and maps) and two wonderful sermon collections by Mark Dever.

With *God's Story in 66 Verses* as part of your spiritual tool kit, I pray that you'll be more knowledgeable, confident, effective, and faithful in handling—and living out—God's Word.

Soli Deo gloria.

OLD TESTAMENT

1

Genesis 15:6

He believed the LORD, and he counted
it to him as righteousness.

THE BIBLE STARTS NOT WITH ADAM AND EVE BUT WITH THE LORD, who creates the universe (Gen. 1:1), setting up the natural (1:3–31) and moral laws (2:16–17) to govern it. Our first parents, however, listen to the serpent and reject God's law in favor of their own (3:1–6), plunging the world and the human race into a cycle of sin and death that continues to this day (3:7–19). But the Lord graciously provides an animal sacrifice to cover our sin (3:21). This promise comes in the context of God's promise of an ultimate Savior who will fatally crush the serpent's head while sustaining a painful wound to himself (3:15).

Pursuing this plan, the Lord saves a reprobate human race ("every intention of the thoughts of his heart was only evil continually" [6:5]) from ultimate destruction in the Flood by providing an ark for Noah and his family (6:6–8). After scattering a dangerously proud humanity at the Tower of Babel (11:1–9), the Lord gets specific in how he will save us. He calls Abram from the pagan land of Babylonia into Canaan, the land bridge of the ancient world, to "bless you and make your name great, so that you will be a blessing" (12:2). Part of God's promise to Abram, who is an old man without an heir, is the provision of offspring as numerous as the stars in the night sky (15:3–5). Abram responds in faith: "He believed the LORD, and [the Lord] counted it to him as righteousness" (15:6).

It is a pivotal moment in the history of salvation, revealing how God graciously deals with his people. The verse and all subsequent salvation history make clear that people are counted righteous by a holy God not on the basis of their good works but on their trusting faith in him. The book of Hebrews says,

> By faith Abraham obeyed when he was called to go out to a place that he was to receive as an inheritance. And he went out, not knowing where he was going. By faith he went to live in the land of promise, as in a foreign land, living in tents with Isaac and Jacob, heirs with him of the same promise. For he was looking forward to the city that has foundations, whose designer and builder is God. (11:8–10)

And God is faithful to his promise to Abraham, providing Isaac as his son (Gen. 21–22) and Jacob and Esau as his grandsons (25). Jacob is a scoundrel who, despite God's promised blessing, cheats his older brother, Esau, out of his birthright (25) and is forced to flee from the promised land, acquiring wives, children, and wealth (28–31). Jacob returns to the land, wrestles with God, and is a changed man (32), finally making peace with Esau (33).

One of Jacob's sons is the precocious and self-confident Joseph, who alienates his jealous, cutthroat brothers and is sold into slavery in Egypt (37). Joseph, with God's hand of blessing, rises to political prominence in Egypt (39–41). Back in Canaan, his brothers are forced by a killer drought to head for Egypt (42:1–5), where Joseph welcomes them (42–50). God has placed Joseph as second in command in Egypt for their protection (50:20). Their descendants, as evidence of God's promise to Abraham, grow into a mighty nation, presenting a strategic problem for Egypt, which eventually will send them back to the land promised to Abraham.

Abraham's faith, credited to him and his descendants as righteousness, is amply rewarded in the history of God's people, who grow into a dynamic kingdom that points the nations to God. When that kingdom falters through the people's unbelief, God remains faithful to them, eventually sending Israel's ultimate King, Jesus Christ. Abraham's faith, credited to him as righteousness, is also a model for the faith in Christ that is required to be in a saving relationship with God:

> No unbelief made [Abraham] waver concerning the promise of God, but he grew strong in his faith as he gave glory to God, fully convinced that God was able to do what he had promised. That is why his faith was "counted to him as righteousness." But the words "it was counted to him" were not written for his sake alone, but for ours also. It will be counted to us who believe in him who raised from the dead Jesus our Lord, who was delivered up for our trespasses and raised for our justification. (Rom. 4:20–25)

As our key verse shows, salvation comes through faith—to Abraham and to us.

2

Exodus 19:5

*If you will indeed obey my voice and keep my
covenant, you shall be my treasured possession
among all peoples, for all the earth is mine.*

THE PEOPLE OF ISRAEL, STARTING WITH ABRAHAM, HAVE RECEIVED
God's promises of a land, a seed (or offspring), and a blessing
(Gen. 12:1–3). Escaping a colossal famine, under the leadership
of Joseph, the fledgling nation is welcomed into the protective
cocoon of Egypt, where it grows into a mighty people after the
patriarchs have passed from the scene (Ex. 1:6–7). Yet the cocoon
is turned into a tomb with the advent of "a new king over Egypt,
who did not know Joseph" (1:8). This pharaoh, fearing for the sta-
bility of his regime, oppresses the Jewish people with hard labor
and a form of genocide, the execution of the male Hebrew children. Yet God protects many of them (1:11–22).

One of the babies who escapes the edict is Moses, and in God's
sovereign plan he grows up as the son of Pharaoh's daughter (2:1–10)
before being driven out as an exile in the land of Midian (2:11–22).
God hears the people's cries for deliverance from Egyptian oppression (2:23–25) and calls Moses to be his instrument (3:1–4:1–17).
A reluctant Moses goes with his brother, Aaron, back to Egypt
and delivers the Lord's command: "Let my people go" (5:1), and

the proud king of Egypt refuses, increasing their burdens. When Moses complains to God, the Lord assures him, "The Egyptians shall know that I am the LORD, when I stretch out my hand against Egypt and bring out the people of Israel from among them" (7:5).

Then the Lord acts, unleashing a series of plagues on Egypt, Egypt's false gods, and a stubborn pharaoh: the Nile turned to blood (7:14–25), frogs from the Nile (8:1–15), dust turned to gnats (8:16–19), flies (8:20–32), the deaths of Egypt's livestock (9:1–7), boils (9:8–12), hail (9:13–35), locusts (10:1–20), darkness (10:21–29), and the deaths of the firstborn (11:1–12:32). In the first Passover, the people who spread the sacrificial blood on their doorposts are spared as the angel of death passes over their homes (12). It is a riveting preview of the substitutionary death of Christ for his people.

Finally, Pharaoh proclaims to Moses, "Up, go out from among my people, both you and the people of Israel; and go, serve the LORD, as you have said. Take your flocks and your herds, as you have said, and be gone, and bless me also!" (12:31–32).

The rejoicing people leave Egypt, instituting the Passover, consecrating their firstborn, and crossing over the Red Sea, while Pharaoh's pursuing hosts are destroyed (14). In the wilderness, Moses sings (15:1–21), but the people begin to complain (15:24–27). Nonetheless God provides bread from heaven (16), water from a rock (which Moses strikes, 17:1–7), and victory over pagan enemies (17:8–16).

The first eighteen chapters of Exodus focus primarily on the escape from Egypt. The second thematic half of the book (chapters 19–40) speaks to the kind of free people the Israelites will be—servers of self and the gods or worshipers of the true Lord of heaven and earth. Thus the book hinges on God's charge in 19:5 and its surrounding verses:

You yourselves have seen what I did to the Egyptians, and how I bore you on eagles' wings and brought you to myself. *Now therefore, if you will indeed obey my voice and keep my covenant, you shall be my treasured possession among all peoples, for all the earth is mine;* and you shall be to me a kingdom of priests and a holy nation. (19:4–6, emphasis added)

The freedom graciously granted to God's people is an invitation not to license but to a life of significance, holiness, beauty, and service. Such a life begins by worshiping the Lord rightly for who he is, and this section focuses on Moses giving the Lord's commands (19–24, including the Ten Commandments [20:1–17]); the Lord's instructions for his portable place of worship, the tabernacle, which the people will use in their travels (25–31); his discipline (32–34); and the construction of his tabernacle as the place to meet him (35–40). The question of Exodus is, will the people obey him?

In Exodus, we see the Creator of heaven and earth graciously save a sinful and thankless people, give them rules for righteous living, prepare them to bless the world, and lay the groundwork for a future Lawgiver, who will also be the ultimate Passover Lamb (1 Cor. 5:7), sacrificing himself for our salvation.

3

Leviticus 11:45

*I am the LORD who brought you up out
of the land of Egypt to be your God. You
shall therefore be holy, for I am holy.*

IN GENESIS, THE LORD CREATES AND CALLS A PEOPLE FOR HIMSELF
in order to bless the world. In Exodus, he rescues them from slavery through Moses and begins instructing them about how he is
to be worshiped. In Leviticus, the Lord tells them what kind of
people he expects them to be. As our pivotal verse says, the people
of God are to be holy because *he* is holy. While in Exodus, Moses
has laid down preliminary rules for God's people to live together
in a holy community and worship him before a watching world; in
Leviticus, he gets specific.

In chapters 1–16, the Israelites, who have not yet entered the
promised land, receive what theologians generally call God's ritual laws. These regulations focus on how God's people, who are
unholy, are to worship their holy Lord. These rituals remind the
people that they are sinful and that access to God is not to be taken
lightly. In Leviticus 1:1–6:7,[1] Moses institutes five offerings: the
burnt offering (for giving thanks or praying), the grain offering
(for praying or praising), the peace offering (for fellowshiping with
the Lord), the sin offering (for repairing one's relationship with
the Lord), and the guilt offering (for repairing one's relationship

with God in more serious matters). Then the Lord instructs the people about how to handle, eat, and dispose of these offerings (6:8–7:38).

The many details in these rituals hammer home the fact that worshiping God is a gracious privilege but is to be done on *his* terms. Because we are sinners, we cannot just come to God in any way we please. But in these chapters God invites us to come to him. These laws show in gracious detail how the Lord's people are to be distinct from the fallen cultures around them so that they can reveal God's holiness and beauty to people who are otherwise lost in darkness.

Chapters 8–10 establish the priesthood: Aaron and his sons are ordained (8), the inaugural service at the tabernacle is celebrated (9), and Aaron's sons are dealt with for worshiping the Lord presumptuously (10).

Chapters 11–15 present laws concerning cleanness and uncleanness. The concept of being clean before the Lord is a physical picture of a moral and spiritual reality. Because God is holy, his people are to be holy. The key verse, 11:45, says this explicitly, linking the command to the historical fact of his gracious salvation from Egyptian bondage.

God's holiness denotes his attribute of moral perfection. The word *holy* basically means to be set apart. God is holy, set apart from sin, and above and beyond his creation, which is fallen because of Adam and Eve's sin. Yet his holiness is communicable to men and women, who are created in his image. We cannot become perfectly holy in this life, but by God's grace we can make holiness our goal and an increasing reality in our lives.

We are to be set apart from the world's sinful patterns in order to save the world and bring glory to our Creator. Ending this first major section of Leviticus, chapter 16 spells out instructions for the Day of Atonement, the holiest day in the Jewish year, in which the high priest enters the Holy of Holies in the tabernacle (and later, the temple) once a year to atone for the sins of the people.

The second main section of Leviticus (17–27) deals most broadly with moral laws but not exclusively. There is much overlap between God's ritual and moral laws, as the Lord seeks to reign in every aspect of the believer's life.

Chapter 17 talks about blood, which is central to the Old Testament sacrificial system. This section anticipates the death of Christ. As Hebrews 9:12 says, "He entered once for all into the holy places, not by means of the blood of goats and calves but by means of his own blood, thus securing an eternal redemption." Chapters 18–22 focus on God's people being holy in comparison to the pagan nations around them and in their own ritual obligations.

Chapter 23 lays out the feasts of Israel: the Sabbath, the Passover, Firstfruits (to celebrate the harvest), Weeks (called pentecost in the New Testament, to recognize the Lord as provider), Trumpets (Rosh Hashanah, the New Year), Atonement, and Booths (release from Egypt). The rest of the book describes other regulations for worship, blasphemy, the years of Sabbath and Jubilee, redemption, and the importance of keeping one's vows.

If the people disobey God's gracious call to holiness, instead of his intended blessings, they will face his curses: "I myself will devastate the land, so that your enemies who settle in it shall be appalled at it. And I will scatter you among the nations, and I will unsheathe the sword after you, and your land shall be a desolation, and your cities shall be a waste" (26:32–33).

Yet God's will is for humanity to glorify and enjoy him forever.[2] Similarly, as Jesus would later say, "Let your light shine before others, so that they may see your good works and give glory to your Father who is in heaven" (Matt. 5:16). Leviticus brings together God's glory with our holiness and joy.

4

Numbers 14:9

Only do not rebel against the LORD. And do not
fear the people of the land, for they are bread
for us. Their protection is removed from them,
and the LORD is with us; do not fear them.

THE LORD HAS BROUGHT THE ISRAELITES TO THE BORDER OF THE
promised land. God is the star in the divine drama; the people
are the supporting cast. Now, however, the Lord takes their
required obedience to a whole new level. He is giving them the
land—but only if they take up arms to win it. The iniquity of
the pagan inhabitants is now complete (Gen. 15:16), and it is
time for the Israelites to show their faith in God by their works
(James 2:14–26). Yet as our key verse shows, they are to do
the work knowing that God is already at work in them (Phil.
2:12–13).

Chapters 1–10 show the Lord preparing the people. In the
wilderness by Mount Sinai, where they have received the Law,
they are numbered in a census (from which comes the English
title of the book) and receive the priests who will serve as media-
tors between God and man (1–4). The camp is cleansed of sin and
uncleanness (5–6), the tabernacle is consecrated and offerings
given (7), the lamps are set up (8:1–4), the Levites are prepared
as priests (8:5–26), the Passover is celebrated (9:1–14), and the

cloud signifying the Lord's presence covers the tabernacle and will go with them (9:15–23).

The scene shifts from Sinai to Kadesh-barnea, on the southern border of the promised land, as the cloud guides them (10). Discord soon arises, however. In chapter 11, the people complain about their troubles and a lack of food, and the Lord responds in righteous anger (kindling a fire) and with grace (providing manna), with Moses showing signs of stress (11:1–15). God arranges helpers for him (11:16–30) and also provides quail as well as a plague on the disobedient (11:31–35). Even Aaron and Miriam, Moses' sister, oppose God's appointed leader, who intercedes for them (12).

It is time to take possession of the land, and the Israelites send twelve spies, only two of whom—Caleb and Joshua—encourage the people that they can prevail with God's help (13). Joshua and Caleb's strong words of faith in 14:9 remind us that faith casts out fear, that God can be completely trusted amid the battles of life. The people give in to their fears and choose faithlessness and rebellion, however, receiving God's judgment: all the people age twenty and older will die in the wilderness after forty years (14:28–35). It is a devastating setback for the Israelites, who have rejected the God who has brought them to the brink of victory. We see their rejection illustrated in the deaths of Korah, Dathan, and Abiram (16).

Yet God's grace never fails. In chapters 20–36, the old, faithless generation—which failed to heed the spy Joshua's warning in 14:9—passes away, replaced by a new generation, ready to act on its faith. The Lord provides for the new generation as the people move from Kadesh to the plains of Moab on the border with the promised land. They are still led by an ancient Moses.

The trials and tests continue: the death of Miriam and another rebellion over a supposed lack of water (20). As in Exodus 17, an exasperated Moses strikes a rock again, although this time the Lord had told him only to *speak to* the rock. As a consequence, Moses will not lead the people into the promised land (Num. 20:12). Perhaps the punishment was so decisive because "the spiritual Rock that followed them . . . was Christ" (1 Cor. 10:4), and Christ was sent to suffer for our sins only at the appointed time. Later in this chapter the king of Edom refuses Israel safe passage (Num. 20:14–21). As the people move on to Mount Hor, Aaron dies, unable to enter the promised land because of his earlier rebellion (20:22–28).

Shortly after the Israelites destroy Arad, they complain about God's provision, and he sends poisonous snakes against them. When the people cry out, God graciously instructs Moses to fashion a bronze serpent and place it on a pole. Those who simply look to it will be saved (21:8–9). The incident prefigures the death of Christ, who said, "As Moses lifted up the serpent in the wilderness, so must the Son of Man be lifted up, that whoever believes in him may have eternal life" (John 3:14–15).

In rapid succession, illustrating Numbers 14:9, the Lord delivers the Israelites from Sihon, Og, and Balak, king of the Midianites, who unsuccessfully summons the pagan prophet Balaam to curse the people of God (21–24). Balaam does, however, provide a remarkable messianic prophecy about "a star [that] shall come out of Jacob" (24:17).

After some final missteps and instructions about life in the promised land (25–36), the new generation is nearly ready to take its inheritance. Yet the question inherent in 14:9 remains for us, their spiritual successors: Will *we* trust God? As Paul said, "Now these things happened to them as an example, but they were written down for our instruction, on whom the end of the ages has come" (1 Cor. 10:11).

5

Deuteronomy 5:29

*Oh that they had such a heart as this always, to fear
me and to keep all my commandments, that it might
go well with them and with their descendants forever!*

AFTER FORTY LONG YEARS, ISRAEL HAS TRAVELED THROUGH FIRE
and water, miracle and misery, to finally stand on the brink of the
promised land, on the other side of the Jordan, on the plains of
Moab. Sinai is in the rearview mirror; Canaan is dead ahead. Yet
Moses has final instructions from the Lord for the people, a second giving of God's law that we call Deuteronomy.

Deuteronomy is the fifth and final book in the Pentateuch.
As such, it provides an important link from the five books of
Moses—with the primeval and patriarchal history of Genesis,
the deliverance of the Jews in Exodus, the laws promulgated
in Leviticus, and the struggles of an unfaithful people in
Numbers—and the coming historical books about the conquest
and settlement of the land.

Deuteronomy contains no action, instead presenting the
three final sermons or speeches of Moses (1:6–4:43; 4:44–26:19;
27–30). The book seems to be written in the form of an ancient
treaty (or covenant) between a king and his people, containing
a historical prologue (1:6–4:43), the laws that the people must
obey (4:44–26:19), and a recitation of blessings and curses for the

people depending on whether they are obedient or disobedient (27–28). The book begins with contextual information (1:1–5) and concludes with Moses' encouragement to the people he will leave behind (29–30) and to Joshua, the new leader (31–34).

Despite (or concurrent with) the book's emphasis on law, the heart of the book is love—both God's love for us and our expected love for him. Our keeping of the Law is seen as an expression of our love for the Lawgiver:

> Hear, O Israel: The LORD our God, the LORD is one. You shall love the LORD your God with all your heart and with all your soul and with all your might. And these words that I command you today shall be on your heart. You shall teach them diligently to your children, and shall talk of them when you sit in your house, and when you walk by the way, and when you lie down, and when you rise. You shall bind them as a sign on your hand, and they shall be as frontlets between your eyes. You shall write them on the doorposts of your house and on your gates.
>
> And when the LORD your God brings you into the land that he swore to your fathers, to Abraham, to Isaac, and to Jacob, to give you—with great and good cities that you did not build, and houses full of all good things that you did not fill, and cisterns that you did not dig, and vineyards and olive trees that you did not plant—and when you eat and are full, then take care lest you forget the LORD, who brought you out of the land of Egypt, out of the house of slavery. It is the LORD your God you shall fear. Him you shall serve and by his name you shall swear. You shall not go after other gods, the gods of the peoples who are around you—for the LORD your God in your midst is a jealous God—lest the anger of the LORD your God be kindled against you, and he destroy you from off the face of the earth. (6:4–15)

We are to love the Lord with everything we have (6:5), and Jesus calls this the Great Commandment (Matt. 22:36–40). Yet we are commanded to love not a brutal, stone-faced taskmaster but a loving Creator. The Lord's love comes before his laws, as our key verse shows: "Oh that they had such a heart as this always, to fear me and to keep all my commandments, that it might go well with them and with their descendants forever!" (Deut. 5:29).

God is not so much after our outward obedience—though this is integral to our spiritual well-being—as he is after our *hearts*. But this is not because he seeks from us a privatized, individualistic faith. The *ESV Study Bible* notes, "The ideal life in the land is for each member of the people, and the body as a whole, to display fervent love to God as their proper response to God's love for them; this is the means by which the rest of the world is to learn of the true God (4:5–8)—the very reason for which Israel exists."[1]

6

Joshua 1:6

*Be strong and courageous, for you shall
cause this people to inherit the land that I
swore to their fathers to give them.*

MOSES WAS A HARD ACT TO FOLLOW, TO SAY THE LEAST. ISRAEL'S
general, lawgiver, and intercessory prayer warrior had stood
with the people through thick and thin, in good times and in
bad, for four decades. We learn from Deuteronomy 34:10–12,
"There has not arisen a prophet since in Israel like Moses, whom
the Lord knew face to face, none like him for all the signs and the
wonders that the Lord sent him to do in the land of Egypt, . . .
and for all the mighty power and all the great deeds of terror that
Moses did in the sight of all Israel."

Yes, "Joshua the son of Nun was full of the spirit of wisdom,
for Moses had laid his hands on him" (34:9), but Moses is now
gone, buried in Moab. Joshua must lead the nation alone. Perhaps
this is why the Lord tells him three times in Joshua 1:6–9 to "be
strong and courageous" (after the same charge has been given by
Moses and the Lord in Deut. 31:6–7, 23).

Joshua faces a seemingly impossible task—to execute the
Lord's judgment on the peoples currently polluting the prom-
ised land. Following pagan gods such as El, Baal, Moloch, and
Asherah, and given over to child sacrifice and to immoral fertility

practices, the inhabitants of the land have reached the end of God's patience, their iniquity finally having reached its "full measure" (see Gen. 15:16 NIV). The Canaanites also must go because their paganism will prove to be a snare to God's people, who must have no other gods (Ex. 20:3–5).

Yet Joshua knows—from the incident with the golden calf to all the complaints in the wilderness—how quickly God's people can turn against their Redeemer. Joshua will indeed need strength and courage. But as the key verse shows, the command comes with the promise that Joshua will succeed:

> Just as I was with Moses, so I will be with you. I will not leave you or forsake you. *Be strong and courageous, for you shall cause this people to inherit the land that I swore to their fathers to give them.* Only be strong and very courageous, being careful to do according to all the law that Moses my servant commanded you. . . . Have I not commanded you? Be strong and courageous. Do not be frightened, and do not be dismayed, for the LORD your God is with you wherever you go. (Josh. 1:5–9, emphasis added)

The book of Joshua describes how its namesake overcame his inherent weakness and fear to defeat God's enemies with God's presence and power. Its chapters can be divided into the following outline:[1]

1–4: *Entrance to the land.* Included are the accounts of a local prostitute named Rahab helping the spies (2) and the crossing of the river Jordan, similar to the Exodus crossing of the Red Sea (3–4).

5: *Consecration and preparation in the land.* The new generation is circumcised, and Passover observed.

6–12: *Conquest of the land.* The fall of Jericho comes in chapter 6 after the people march around the city and blow their horns. Rahab is spared, proving that the book is not about an ancient campaign of ethnic cleansing. Ai is destroyed after the sin of Achan is exposed and paid for (7–8). Israel is tricked into sparing Gibeon (9). The Lord fights for Israel, the sun stands still, and much of Canaanite territory, south and north, falls to the Jews (10–12).

13–22: *Division of the land.* Territory is allotted east (13) and west (14) of the Jordan for the tribes of Judah (15), Ephraim and Manasseh (16–17), Benjamin (18), Simeon, Zebulun, Issachar, Asher, Naphtali, and Dan, as well as lands given to Joshua (19). Cities of refuge are established for those who kill accidentally (20). Levi, which has no land of its own, receives cities and lands in the other tribal lands (21). Reuben, Gad, and the half tribe of Manasseh, having been granted territory east of the Jordan (Num. 32), now return to their land, having fulfilled their responsibilities (Josh. 22).

23–24: *Closing instructions in the land.* Joshua, "old and well advanced in years" (23:2), calls on the leaders of the nation to be faithful, reminding them that "not one word has failed of all the good things that the LORD your God promised concerning you" (23:14). God will continue saving them. Joshua says, "If it is evil in your eyes to serve the LORD, choose this day whom you will serve. . . . But as for me and my house, we will serve the LORD" (24:15).

In the looming absence of Joshua, now it is the people of God who must be strong and courageous. Those who follow the ultimate Savior, Jesus Christ, must do likewise until he returns.

7

Judges 8:34

*The people of Israel did not remember the
Lord their God, who had delivered them from
the hand of all their enemies on every side.*

AFTER ALL THE WANDERINGS OF THE PATRIARCHS, AFTER FOUR
hundred years in Egypt, after forty years in the wilderness,
the people of God have conquered much—but not all—of the
promised land. It would be nice to end the story here with the
comforting words, "And they lived happily ever after." But Judges,
the second of the Bible's historical books, is no fairy tale. The
Lord leaves some of the Canaanites in the land to discipline and
test them (2:20–23; 3:4).

In distressing detail, Judges recounts Israel's repeated falls
into apostasy, its devastation at the hands of foreign enemies, its
cries for help, the Lord's gracious provision of a judge, its time
of rest, and its fall again into sin. Without a strong leader such as
Moses or Joshua, the people show the true state of their faith—
or lack thereof. As the key verse says, "The people of Israel did
not remember the Lord their God, who had delivered them
from the hand of all their enemies on every side" (8:34). God
was forgotten but not gone.

Chapter 2:15–19 summarizes the dynamic of this spiritual
dark age:

Whenever they marched out, the hand of the LORD was against them for harm, as the LORD had warned, and as the LORD had sworn to them. And they were in terrible distress.

Then the LORD raised up judges, who saved them out of the hand of those who plundered them. Yet they did not listen to their judges, for they whored after other gods and bowed down to them. They soon turned aside from the way in which their fathers had walked, who had obeyed the commandments of the LORD, and they did not do so. Whenever the LORD raised up judges for them, the LORD was with the judge, and he saved them from the hand of their enemies all the days of the judge. For the LORD was moved to pity by their groaning because of those who afflicted and oppressed them. But whenever the judge died, they turned back and were more corrupt than their fathers, going after other gods, serving them and bowing down to them. They did not drop any of their practices or their stubborn ways.

This statement in our key verse, they "did not remember the LORD their God," indicates spiritual amnesia of a high order.

The book describes how the nation failed to complete the conquest (1), fell into disobedience and received the Lord's discipline after the death of Joshua (2:1–15), and needed the judges (2:16–3:6). Then the book details the challenges and exploits of the various judges:

3:7–11: Othniel defeats Cushan-rishathaim.

3:12–30: Ehud defeats a "very fat" Eglon and Moab.

3:31: Shamgar kills six hundred Philistines with an oxgoad.

4–5: Deborah, the lone female judge, defeats Jabin, the king of Canaan, with the woman Jael's strategic use of a tent peg into the head of the pagan commander Sisera.

6–8: Gideon resists and then accepts the Lord's call (6), defeats Midian with three hundred men (7), kills two Midianite kings (8:1–21), makes an ephod—a religious image—that becomes a stumbling block to the people (8:22–28), and dies (8:29–35), with the people forgetting the Lord once again.

9: Gideon's son Abimelech is made king through violence and intrigue before being killed.

10:1–5: Tola and Jair judge Israel.

10:6–12:7: Jephthah delivers a sinful and oppressed Israel from the Ammonites, kills his daughter because of a foolish vow, and fights the men of Ephraim (who could not pronounce "Shibboleth").

12:8–15: Ibzan, Elon, and Abdon judge Israel.

13–16: Samson is born (13), gets married (14), defeats a thousand Philistines with a donkey's jawbone (15), falls in love with and is betrayed by a Philistine woman named Delilah (16:1–22), and ultimately slaughters the Philistines (16:23–31): "So the dead whom he killed at his death were more than those whom he had killed during his life" (16:30).

If it is possible, the end of the book is even more depressing:

17–18: *Idolatry.* Micah hires a Levite (17), who is taken by the tribe of Dan, which worshiped a metal image that the priest had made (18). Twice we are told in these chapters that "there was no king in Israel."

19–21: *Rape, murder, and war.* A Levite's concubine is murdered by "worthless" Benjaminites in a scene reminiscent of Sodom (Gen. 19); the Levite cuts up his concubine (Judg. 19) to rouse the people; and Israel starts a civil war with Benjamin (20) and provides wives for the surviving men of Benjamin (21).

The theme of leaderless anarchy is punctuated at the end of the book: "In those days, there was no king in Israel. Everyone did what was right in his own eyes" (21:25). The people have forgotten all that the Lord has done for them and need a godly king to help set things right.

8

Ruth 1:16

*Ruth said, "Do not urge me to leave you or to
return from following you. For where you go I will
go, and where you lodge I will lodge. Your people
shall be my people, and your God my God."*

IN THE MIDST OF THE DARKNESS AND DEGRADATION OF THE JUDGES ERA, THE
book of Ruth is, as John Piper says, "a love story . . . the portrait
of beautiful, noble manhood and womanhood."[1] However, Ruth's
background as a native of Moab left little reason for optimism:

- The nation was founded through the illicit union of Lot
  and one of Lot's daughters (Gen. 19:30–38).
- As with the Ammonites, the people of Moab were
  prohibited from entering the assembly of the Lord
  (Deut. 23:3).
- Like Edom, they refused Israel passage to the promised
  land and hired the false prophet Balaam to curse Israel
  (Num. 21–24).
- The Israelite judge Ehud assassinated the repulsive
  Moabite king, Eglon (Judg. 3:12–30).
- Moab's chief god, Chemosh (meaning "destroyer,"
  "subduer," or "fish god"), demanded human sacrifice.[2]

How did we go from a cursed culture to perhaps the pre-eminent love story in all of ancient literature? It starts with God's providence. If the wars and massacres of Joshua and Judges are hard to come to terms with, the excruciating hand that God dealt to Naomi, a Jewish woman, is no less so.

A famine forces Naomi, her husband, Elimelech, and their sons, Mahlon and Chilion, to flee the promised land for hated Moab. Yet the calamities mount. Elimelech dies. The young men eventually take two local women, named Orpah and Ruth, as their wives, but then Naomi's sons die (1:1–5). Finally, bereft of her husband and sons, Naomi decides to return to Israel, since the famine has finally ended. She bids her two daughters-in-law to remain in their homeland to begin new lives. One, Orpah, reluctantly agrees. The other, Ruth, the widow of Mahlon, makes a fateful decision to cleave to Naomi and to Naomi's God, come what may:

> Ruth said, "Do not urge me to leave you or to return from follow-ing you. For where you go I will go, and where you lodge I will lodge. Your people shall be my people, and your God my God. Where you die I will die, and there will I be buried. May the LORD do so to me and more also if anything but death parts me from you." (1:16–17, emphasis added)

In the face of inexplicable losses from the Lord's hand, Ruth makes a decision that will change her life—and the world. Ruth goes with Naomi to start over (1:19–22). Despite this act of com-mitment and kindness, grieving Naomi is angry at God. She tells the women of her hometown, Bethlehem, to stop calling her Naomi, which means "pleasant," and instead call her Mara, which means "bitter." She and Ruth have next to nothing, and so Ruth goes into the fields of a distant, wealthy relative named Boaz to glean grain (Lev. 19:9–10; Deut. 24:19), and he treats her with special kindness (Ruth 2:1–17).

Naomi finds out and encourages what she sees as a fledgling romance (2:18–3:5). Taking her eyes off herself and placing them onto someone else is the start of Naomi's spiritual and emotional restoration. Ruth follows her instructions and elicits a pledge from the older man, struck by her "kindness" to him (3:10), that he will seek to "redeem" (3:13) her through marriage, according to the custom. Naomi tells Ruth confidently, "Wait, my daughter, until you learn how the matter turns out, for the man will not rest but will settle the matter today" (3:18).

And indeed Boaz *does* redeem Ruth, a poor woman from Moab (4:1–12). They get married and have a child, named Obed, "a restorer of life and a nourisher of [Naomi's] old age" (4:15). Drenched in the Lord's kindness, Naomi experiences the return of her joy. Then the narrator fills in the significance of Obed's birth: "He was the father of Jesse, the father of David" (4:17).

Soon Israel, stumbling from one judge to the next, would have its godly king—all because a Moabite woman chose God and God's people. This king would set the standard for the nation until a greater son of David would be born one night in a stable in Bethlehem (Matt. 1:1; 2:1).

9

1 Samuel 2:35

I will raise up for myself a faithful priest, who shall do according to what is in my heart and in my mind. And I will build him a sure house, and he shall go in and out before my anointed forever.

ISRAEL'S LONG, DARK ERA BETWEEN THE CONQUEST AND THE monarchy was filled with ruffians and rogues, including many of the judges, such as Gideon and Samson. But 1 Samuel injects a hopeful note. The judges are passing from the scene; a king is finally coming.

The book opens with Elkanah and his two wives (1:1–8). One, Peninnah, is blessed with children, while the other, Hannah, is barren. Vying for their husband's love, Peninnah provokes Hannah to tears. Elkanah asks, "Hannah, why do you weep? And why do you not eat? And why is your heart sad? Am I not more to you than ten sons?" (1:8).

In her anguish, Hannah pours out her heart in prayer at the temple in Shiloh, a precursor to the yet-to-be-built temple in Jerusalem (1:9–18). At first, the priest, Eli, surmises that she is drunk but then learns her plight and kindly dismisses her with the words, "Go in peace, and the God of Israel grant your petition" (1:17). In time, the Lord gives Hannah a son, Samuel (1:19–20), and she in turn gives him back to the Lord to serve as a priest, under the tutelage of Eli (1:21–28).

The parallels between young Samuel and the coming of Jesus Christ three millennia in the future are numerous. Both are conceived in remarkable ways—Hannah is barren while Mary is a virgin (Matt. 1:18–25). Hannah's great prayer of thanks to the Lord who "lifts the needy from the ash heap" (1 Sam. 2:1–10) complements Mary's later Magnificat to the Lord, who "has looked on the humble estate of his servant" (Luke 1:46–55). The boy Samuel serves in the temple (1 Sam. 3), while Jesus was in his "Father's house" (Luke 2:41–51). Samuel, we are told, "continued to grow both in stature and in favor with the LORD and also with man" (1 Sam. 2:26). Jesus, for his part, "increased in wisdom and in stature and in favor with God and man" (Luke 2:52). Jesus was Israel's ultimate son of David, yet Samuel pointed to David, the nation's greatest earthly king.

Eli's time as judge is coming to an inglorious end, with his two sons using their positions to exploit the people (1 Sam. 2:12–25). A prophet tells Eli that the end is near, adding, "I will raise up for myself a faithful priest, who shall do according to what is in my heart and in my mind. And I will build him a sure house, and he shall go in and out before my anointed forever" (2:35). This verse is the fulcrum for the book. The faithful priest is Samuel, who will serve the anointed king and, ultimately, the Messiah (which means "anointed").

The rest of 1 Samuel fleshes out the transition from Samuel to Israel's monarchy. Samuel is called (3), Samuel is installed as judge (7), the people cry out for a king (8:1–9), and the Lord grants their demand over Samuel's misgivings (8:10–22). Samuel is unhappy, but the Lord tells him, "Listen to all that the people are saying to you; it is not you they have rejected, but they have rejected me as their king" (8:7 NIV).

A handsome, tall, but shy young man named Saul is chosen as king (9). Samuel anoints him (10), instructing the new king to wait for one week at a town called Gilgal. Samuel then proclaims Saul to be Israel's king.

In chapter 13, however, Saul's character is revealed. He refuses to wait for Samuel at Gilgal and rashly offers a sacrifice, only to lie about it. Samuel pronounces judgment. "You have done foolishly," he says. "The LORD has sought out a man after his own heart, and the LORD has commanded him to be prince over his people, because you have not kept what the LORD commanded you" (13:13–14).

The man after God's own heart is David. The rest of the book depicts the agonizing fall of Saul and the inexorable rise of the shepherd boy from Bethlehem, who embodies the faith that God requires. "For the LORD sees not as man sees," God tells Samuel, "man looks on the outward appearance, but the LORD looks on the heart" (16:7).

David's heart for the Lord is evident through life's trials. David slays a giant (17); loves Jonathan, the son of his rival (18); spares Saul not once but twice (24, 26); and is a mighty warrior for his Lord (31). After the death of Saul, the way is clear for the Lord's new anointed to give Israel a glimpse of what a godly king should be—until the arrival of the ultimate King.

10

2 Samuel 7:16

*Your house and your kingdom shall be made sure forever
before me. Your throne shall be established forever.*

THE BIBLE, FROM GENESIS TO REVELATION, DOESN'T PRESENT GOD
as aloof and unknowable but as a loving heavenly Father. This
God ardently desires not just our obedience but *us*. He walks with
Adam and Eve in the garden until sin ruptures the relationship.
Scripture's final book portrays a loud voice crying from the heavenly throne, "Behold, the dwelling place of God is with man. He
will dwell with them, and they will be his people, and God himself will be with them as their God" (Rev. 21:3).

This theme of the Lord's loving presence is crystallized in the
idea of Israel's king. Since the time an ancient Jacob prophesied
about a "scepter" coming from the tribe of Judah (Gen. 49:10)
and Balaam saw "a star [that] shall come out of Jacob" (Num.
24:17), Israel longed for a king to lead them in the ways of God.
This king would be a living embodiment of God's rule, care, and
protection for his people.

Israel's first encounter with a monarch was a short-lived but
tragic disaster, however. As 1 Samuel shows with brutal honesty,
Saul was fatally flawed, putting his interests above God's. Rather
than yield the throne to David, a better man whom he knows
will supplant him, Saul seeks David's life again and again. So the

kingdom is torn from Saul, who dies with three of his sons on Mount Gilboa (31:8). The people are scattered, like sheep without a shepherd.

Second Samuel shows how David received the kingship, setting the standard for all Israel's future rulers and calling forth a people's messianic hope. That hope was given substance through what theologians call the Davidic covenant, God's promise that he would establish David and his descendants over Israel forever:

> I took you from the pasture, from following the sheep, that you should be prince over my people Israel. . . . And I will appoint a place for my people Israel and will plant them, so that they may dwell in their own place and be disturbed no more. And violent men shall afflict them no more, as formerly, from the time that I appointed judges over my people Israel. And I will give you rest from all your enemies. Moreover, the LORD declares to you that the LORD will make you a house. When your days are fulfilled and you lie down with your fathers, I will raise up your offspring after you, who shall come from your body, and I will establish his kingdom. He shall build a house for my name, and I will establish the throne of his kingdom forever. I will be to him a father, and he shall be to me a son. When he commits iniquity, I will discipline him with the rod of men, with the stripes of the sons of men, but my steadfast love will not depart from him, as I took it from Saul, whom I put away from before you. *And your house and your kingdom shall be made sure forever before me. Your throne shall be established forever.* (2 Sam. 7:8–16, emphasis added)

Although the promise of the kingship is everlasting, King David has to consolidate it in the here and now. He quickly conquers Canaanite-controlled Jerusalem, making it Israel's political and religious capital, transferring the ark of the covenant there from Kiriath-jearim (6). Later, he will provide for the building of the temple in Jerusalem, which his son Solomon will complete.

David removes the Philistines from the hill country (5:17–25), vanquishes Moab (8:2), and conquers the Syrians (8:3–8) and Edom (8:13–14). David stretches Israel's borders all the way to the Euphrates in the north and to Edom in the south. Under David, Israel controls nearly all the land promised by God.

Throughout these events, David displays humility and trust in his Lord, writing many of the psalms, forming the core of the nation's hymnal. But despite the promise of a sure kingdom, David makes horrible choices that undercut his forty-year rule. He commits adultery with Bathsheba and murders her husband, Uriah the Hittite, to cover it up (11). Staying true to the covenant, God nonetheless is gracious, calling David to repentance (12). But his rule is diminished from then on.

An awful episode of incestuous rape by his foolish son Amnon is followed by murder and intrigue (13–14). His treasonous son Absalom forces David to flee the City of David for a time (15–19). In the north, a "worthless" Benjaminite named Sheba attempts to claim the kingship (20). David also sins by taking a census (24).

Although Israel's greatest king stumbles repeatedly, the Lord's covenant faithfulness never wavers. His promise, "Your throne shall be established forever," finds fulfillment in Jesus Christ, the ultimate "son of David" (Matt. 1:1), who "became flesh and dwelt among us" (John 1:14).

11

1 Kings 11:11

The LORD said to Solomon, "Since this has been your practice and you have not kept my covenant and my statutes that I have commanded you, I will surely tear the kingdom from you and will give it to your servant."

FIRST KINGS OPENS WITH A SICKLY DAVID NEAR DEATH AND ONE OF his sons, Adonijah, attempting to seize power. David responds by throwing his support to Solomon, his son with Bathsheba (1). David then instructs his successor to settle scores with his enemies Adonijah, Joab, and Shimei. Solomon does so after they reveal their true colors (2).

The narrative assumes, however, a more exalted tone in chapter 3. The Lord appears to the new king in a dream, saying, "Ask what I shall give you" (3:5). Solomon asks for wisdom, not wealth or power (3:7–9), and the Lord, pleased by this wise answer, gives him "wisdom and understanding beyond measure, and breadth of mind like the sand on the seashore, so that Solomon's wisdom surpassed the wisdom of all the people of the east and all the wisdom of Egypt. For he was wiser than all other men . . . and his fame was in all the surrounding nations. He also spoke 3,000 proverbs, and his songs were 1,005" (4:29–32).

God's people, in partial fulfillment of the promise to Abraham (Gen. 12:1–3), are now blessing the nations. The queen of Sheba visits Solomon, declaring, "The report was true that I heard in my own land of your words and of your wisdom, but I did not believe the reports until I came and my own eyes had seen it. And behold, the half was not told me. . . . Blessed be the LORD your God, who has delighted in you and set you on the throne of Israel!" (1 Kings 10:6–7, 9).

"Judah and Israel were as many as the sand by the sea," the author of 1 Kings informs us. "They ate and drank and were happy" (4:20). We see Solomon's wisdom with the two women and the baby (3:16–28), in his wealth (4:21–28; 7:1–12; 8:62–66; 10:14–29), in his preparations and provisions for the massive temple (5–6; 7:13–8:21, 62–66), and in his godly blessing and prayer after the temple is finally constructed (8:12–61). The people now have a permanent place to worship the Lord. The objective is "that all the peoples of the earth may know that the LORD is God; there is no other" (8:60).

Yet the Lord's model kingdom falls apart quickly. The Lord has given Solomon a conditional promise: "*If* you will walk before me, as David your father walked, . . . *then* I will establish your royal throne over Israel forever, as I promised David your father. . . . But *if* you turn aside from following me, . . . *then* I will cut off Israel from the land that I have given them, and the house that I have consecrated for my name I will cast out of my sight" (9:4–7, emphasis added).

Shockingly, Solomon, the wisest of all men, turns aside. He allows his many foreign wives to turn away "his heart after other gods" (11:4). And God, true to his word, promises Solomon that judgment is coming: "I will surely tear the kingdom from you and will give it to your servant" (11:11).

That servant is Jeroboam, who becomes king over the ten northern tribes (hereafter known as Israel) when Solomon's foolish son and successor, Rehoboam, refuses to lighten the people's load (11:26–12:24). Rehoboam is left only with Judah. But despite God's offer of blessing (11:30–38), Jeroboam fears he will lose the people's allegiance if they worship in Jerusalem, so he sets up pagan worship sites in the north (12:25–33). It is an archetypal act that becomes known as "the sin of Jeroboam."

Thus starts a downward cycle in both the Northern and the Southern Kingdoms. The northern kings are uniformly bad, while the kings of Judah are a mixed lot, most of them far below the caliber of David. The Lord sends prophets to call kings and people to repent, showing his sovereign power, grace, and judgment (13–14, 20, 22). Yet the people are lukewarm, hedging their bets.

Elijah alternately stares down and flees from evil King Ahab and Queen Jezebel and receives the Lord's gracious provision throughout (17–19). In a showdown with 450 priests of Baal on Mount Carmel (18:20–40), Elijah cries out to the people, "How long will you go limping between two different opinions? If the LORD is God, follow him; but if Baal, then follow him" (18:21).

Too often in 1 Kings, the people, their grand kingdom shattered, make the wrong choice.

12

2 Kings 17:13

*Yet the LORD warned Israel and Judah by every prophet
and every seer, saying, "Turn from your evil ways and
keep my commandments and my statutes, in accordance
with all the Law that I commanded your fathers, and
that I sent to you by my servants the prophets."*

AFTER THE EARLIER HISTORICAL BOOKS OF THE BIBLE DEPICTED THE
rise of the Jewish empire, the book of 2 Kings depicts its ugly fall,
in both Israel (the Northern Kingdom) and Judah (the Southern
Kingdom). "When we look at 1 and 2 Samuel and 1 and 2 Kings
together," says Mark Dever, "the overall thesis is ironic, but clear:
the nation that Joshua led into Canaan to be a witness to the surrounding nations becomes instead an imitation of those nations.…
And because the people have become just another nation, the story
ends with Judah in exile and dispersed among the nations."[1]

In 2 Kings we see a grim downward spiral and also signs of
the Lord's continuing grace and care. Those signs come embod-
ied in the lives of the prophets, who seek to stop the people from
careening over the spiritual cliff. If Elijah was the main prophetic
figure in 1 Kings, his protégé, Elisha, takes center stage in this
book (2:1–10:36).

After Elijah is translated to heaven (2:9–12), Elisha receives
a double portion of his master's spirit, parting the waters of the

Jordan and crossing into the troubled promised land (2:14), emulating Moses (who parted the Red Sea [Ex. 14]) and Joshua (who
crossed the river [Josh. 3]).[2] The nation's new standard-bearer
will need all the miracles he can get. The Lord works a series of
wonders through Elisha, among them:

- A widow escapes financial ruin (and her sons' slavery) by
  selling oil that multiplies in her household vessels (4:1–7,
  reminiscent of Jesus' multiplying loaves and fish).
- A barren woman from Shunem and her husband are
  blessed with a son, who is later brought back to life
  (4:8–37, reminiscent of the miraculous birth of John the
  Baptist and the raising of Lazarus).
- During a famine, some poisonous stew is made safe
  (4:38–41, perhaps a reminder of the Bread of Life).
- A hundred men are fed with a small number of loaves,
  fruit, and grain (4:42–44, similar to the feedings of the
  five thousand and the three thousand).
- Naaman, a Syrian commander, is healed of leprosy and
  converted (5:1–14, 18), though the servant Gehazi's greed
  is punished with leprosy (5:15–27; see the passage with
  Jesus and the ten lepers in Luke 17).
- An axe head floats, saving an acolyte from indebtedness
  (6:1–7, reminds us of Jesus' words in Matt. 6:8: "Your
  Father knows what you need before you ask him").
- The Syrian army is confounded and gently sent home
  (6:8–23, reminds us of Jesus' words in Matt. 5:44: "Love
  your enemies").

But the prophets also speak judgment. Elisha sends an appren-
tice to anoint Jehu as king of Israel and to destroy the house of Ahab
and Jezebel (2 Kings 9:1–10:17) for killing the prophets in Elijah's

day (1 Kings 18:4). Jehu also strikes down the prophets of Baal (2 Kings 10:18–27). However, "Jehu was not careful to walk in the law of the LORD, the God of Israel, with all his heart" (10:31). The result: "In those days the LORD began to cut off parts of Israel" (10:32).

Eventually, the mighty Assyrian army arrives at the gates of Samaria, the capital, and captures it, deporting the Jews across the pagan empire, outside the promised land (17:6) in 722 BC.

As the Assyrian army moves south and surrounds Jerusalem, a spokesman for King Sennacherib taunts, "Who among all the gods of the lands have delivered their lands out of my hand, that the LORD should deliver Jerusalem out of my hand?" (18:35). Yet the Lord *does* deliver. With the encouragement of the prophet Isaiah, good King Hezekiah refuses to surrender. The Lord rewards his trust, saying, "I will defend this city to save it, for my own sake and for the sake of my servant David" (19:34). That night the angel of the Lord strikes down 185,000 soldiers. The rest beat a hasty retreat (19:35–37).

Yet the reprieve for Judah is short-lived. Hezekiah stumbles, revealing the nation's wealth to Babylonian envoys (20). Manasseh, his evil successor, plunges Judah to new spiritual depths (21). Despite a brief renaissance of righteousness through good King Josiah (22–23), Judah forgets God and eventually faces disaster at the hands of Nebuchadnezzar, who captures Jerusalem and destroys the temple (25) in 586 BC.

As our key verse says, the people failed to turn from their "evil ways" (17:13), and the result was terrifying judgment. Like Israel, Judah ultimately falls because it has failed to repent at the prophets' many warnings (17:13). Disaster overtook both kingdoms because God's people—ignoring God's repeated warnings—chose God's judgments over his blessings. For Judah, the downward spiral was complete. God's kingdom had failed.

Or had it?

13

1 Chronicles 29:18

*O LORD, the God of Abraham, Isaac, and Israel, our
fathers, keep forever such purposes and thoughts in the
hearts of your people, and direct their hearts toward you.*

THE BOOKS OF 1 AND 2 CHRONICLES—INITIALLY PARTS OF A SINGLE
work—cover the same ground as the earlier historical books
2 Samuel and 1 and 2 Kings. It would be a mistake, however,
to treat the Chronicles as spiritual reruns. The Septuagint, the
influential Greek translation of the Old Testament that circulated
during Jesus' time, called the combined work *Paraleipomena*, or
"'the things omitted,' indicating that it was considered a supplement to the books of Samuel and Kings."[1]

In the stream of Old Testament history, Chronicles was written near the end. David assumed the kingship around 1000 BC,
the nation split in 931, the Northern Kingdom was conquered
by Assyria in 722, Judah fell to Babylon in 586, Babylon fell to
Persia in 538, Jews began returning to the promised land in 538
under the decree of Cyrus, a smaller temple was rebuilt in 516, the
scribe Ezra returned in 458 to reestablish the Law, and Nehemiah
returned in 445 to rebuild Jerusalem's walls.[2]

Scholars believe Chronicles to be the work of priests and
scribes to encourage the Jewish people who had returned from
exile in the Persian Empire. We will treat Chronicles here as two

biblical books, as it appears in our English Bibles, knowing that initially it was one work.

In 1 Chronicles, the postexilic Jewish people have a parallel account of Israel's history, starting with Adam, the head of the entire human race, and going all the way through the reign of David (1:1–29:30). This linkage drives home the point that the Jews are blessed to be a blessing *to the nations* (Gen. 12:1–3). In a real sense, the story of Israel is *our* story, too, whatever our tribe.

The first eight chapters are mainly genealogies of the tribes of Israel, from Judah through Benjamin. Israel, though torn from the land because of its disobedience, has deep roots there. First Chronicles 9 brings us to the present, detailing those who first returned to Jerusalem (9:1–34), taking special notice of priests, Levites, and temple servants. Clearly, worship is on the people's minds, even though the temple and their numbers are far smaller than before.

Worship of the covenant-making God remains at the forefront of 1 Chronicles. After a brief recitation of the line of Saul (9:35–44), the first king, the book changes its approach from primarily genealogy to narrative, as David, the ideal king, steps onstage. Without recounting David's personal foibles, 1 Chronicles depicts his inexorable rise to power over the unfaithful Saul (10:1–12:40), for "all the rest of Israel were of a single mind to make David king.... [And] there was joy in Israel" (12:38, 40).

Then the author describes in great detail David's transporting the ark of the covenant—the preeminent symbol of God's presence and the ritual focus of the Mosaic covenant—from Kiriath-jearim (13). After a brief interlude about David's family and defeat of the Philistines (14), we return to the ark. It is carefully brought to Jerusalem "with rejoicing. . . . So all Israel brought up the ark of the covenant of the LORD with shouting, to the sound of the horn, trumpets, and cymbals, and made loud music on harps and lyres" (15:25, 28). When the ark is placed in a tent (16), David leads the congregation in a song of thanksgiving that includes this closing prayer:

> Save us, O God of our salvation,
>   and gather and deliver us from among the nations,
> that we may give thanks to your holy name
>   and glory in your praise.
> Blessed be the LORD, the God of Israel,
>   from everlasting to everlasting! (16:35–36)

It is a prayer for all seasons—when David is king, when the people are in exile among the nations, and when Christ's followers eagerly await their Savior King's return.

Chapter 17 recounts the Davidic covenant (see the chapter in this book on 2 Samuel) before the narrative returns to David's exploits and actions (18–21, 27) and his preparations for the temple to come (22–26, 28–29). True worship of the covenant-keeping God is marked not only by right actions but also by right attitudes. The king acknowledges this timeless truth in his prayer:

> I know, my God, that you test the heart and have pleasure in uprightness. In the uprightness of my heart I have freely offered all these things, and now I have seen your people, who are present here, offering freely and joyously to you. O LORD, the God of Abraham, Isaac, and Israel, our fathers, keep forever such purposes and thoughts in the hearts of your people, and direct their hearts toward you. (29:17–18, emphasis added)

True worship, as taught in both Testaments (Isa. 1:14–20; John 4:23), springs from the heart.

14

2 Chronicles 7:14

If my people who are called by my name humble
themselves, and pray and seek my face and turn
from their wicked ways, then I will hear from heaven
and will forgive their sin and heal their land.

FOR DECADES, AMERICAN EVANGELICALS HAVE BEEN FOND OF quoting 2 Chronicles 7:14 as a means of national renewal. The famous verse, however, comes in the context of a book that has a bigger message: God's covenant-keeping mercy triumphs over his covenant-induced judgment, even when all hope seems lost.

Chronicles, as we noted in the last chapter, was written for Jews who were returning to the promised land after seventy years of exile. For Israel, the promise of 7:14 "includes deliverance from drought and pestilence as well as the return of exiles to their rightful home. . . . [And] the restoration of the people to their right relationship with God."[1] So even though the book recounts much of the same dreary decline as does 2 Kings, ultimately 2 Chronicles is a book of hope.

In keeping with this theme, 2 Chronicles ignores the decline and fall of Israel, the Northern Kingdom, overthrown by Assyria in 722 BC. Despite the gracious presence of prophets such as Elijah and Elisha, Israel was apostate from the beginning and was judged permanently. There was no more grace available, no more lessons for its inhabitants to learn.

Not so for Judah, the Southern Kingdom. True, Nebuchadnezzar smashed Jerusalem and the temple in 586 BC and carried off Daniel and thousands more into exile. But God had promised to return them to the land (Dan. 9:24) and, ultimately, to send the Messiah, in David's line (Hag. 2:23). Second Chronicles, written for their descendants (and us), is replete with encouragement for all those exiles who are called "my people."

The temple, where God formally meets his people, remains in the forefront of the narrative. The first nine chapters cover its preparation (1:1–2:18), building (3:1–5:1), and dedication (5:2–7:22), followed by the rest of Solomon's achievements (8–9). The king's personal characteristics are ignored. He functions as God's chosen king under the Davidic covenant (2 Sam. 7; 1 Chron. 17). After the temple is dedicated, the Lord appears to Solomon at night, offering both a carrot and a stick:

> I have heard your prayer and have chosen this place for myself as a house of sacrifice. When I shut up the heavens so that there is no rain, or command the locust to devour the land, or send pestilence among my people, *if my people who are called by my name humble themselves, and pray and seek my face and turn from their wicked ways, then I will hear from heaven and will forgive their sin and heal their land.* Now my eyes will be open and my ears attentive to the prayer that is made in this place. . . . And as for you, if you will walk before me as David your father walked, . . . then I will establish your royal throne. . . .
>
> But if you turn aside and forsake my statutes and my commandments that I have set before you, and go and serve other gods and worship them, then I will pluck you up from my land that I have given you, and this house that I have consecrated for my name, I will cast out of my sight, and I will make it a

proverb and a byword among all peoples. (2 Chron. 7:12–20, emphasis added)

These words would have special resonance for Israel's postexilic community—and for all who have faced the Lord's discipline (Heb. 12:7–11). Despite the Lord's words, however, the balance of the book portrays Judah's steady march into idolatry and disaster (2 Chron. 10–36).

Yet 2 Chronicles ends on a hopeful note:

Now in the first year of Cyrus king of Persia, that the word of the LORD by the mouth of Jeremiah might be fulfilled, the LORD stirred up the spirit of Cyrus king of Persia, so that he made a proclamation throughout all his kingdom and also put it in writing: "Thus says Cyrus king of Persia, 'The LORD, the God of heaven, has given me all the kingdoms of the earth, and he has charged me to build him a house at Jerusalem, which is in Judah. Whoever is among you of all his people, may the LORD his God be with him. Let him go up.'" (36:22–23)

Israel, blessed to be a blessing to the nations (Gen. 12:1–3), finds itself blessed *by* the nations. The Lord's work of forgiveness and healing has begun.

15

Ezra 9:14

*Shall we break your commandments again
and intermarry with the peoples who practice
these abominations? Would you not be angry
with us until you consumed us, so that there
should be no remnant, nor any to escape?*

THE BOOK OF EZRA TELLS THE STORY OF GOD'S FAITHFULNESS EVEN
when his people are doubly unfaithful. Judah finds its once proud
kingdom, meant to draw the nations to the Lord, smashed by
those nations—specifically by Nebuchadnezzar, king of Babylon,
in the destruction of Jerusalem in 586 BC.

Yet God's faithfulness supersedes his wrath. When the punishment is completed, the surviving Jewish exiles, now subject to
Gentile rule, return by decree of Cyrus of Persia. Ezra recounts
several returns into the promised land over about a century. The
people are no longer free or wealthy, but they can again worship
the Lord. Ezra appears toward the end of this period, reminding
his fellow Jews that orthodoxy (right doctrine) and orthopraxy
(right practice) must go together.

The book initially was one work with Nehemiah in the Hebrew
canon.[1] Chapters 1:1–2:70 describe the proclamation of Cyrus
in 538 and the resulting return of the exiles. Chapters 3–6 cover
the rebuilding of the temple's foundation (3), opposition by local

enemies (4), the resumption of the work under Zerubbabel the son of Shealtiel and Jeshua the son of Jozadak (5), and the re-affirmation of the decree and completion of the temple in 516 (6). All this happens before Ezra shows up.

The rebuilding, though an answer to prayer, is on a much smaller scale than Solomon's temple: "Many of the priests and Levites and heads of fathers' houses, old men who had seen the first house, wept with a loud voice when they saw the foundation of this house being laid, though many shouted aloud for joy, so that the people could not distinguish the sound of the joyful shout from the sound of the people's weeping" (3:12–13).

Ezra, described as "a scribe skilled in the Law of Moses" and as someone who "had set his heart to study the Law of the LORD . . . and to teach his statutes and rules in Israel" (7:6, 10), is sent from Babylon in 458 by King Artaxerxes to teach the people the Word of God (7). Ezra is thrilled with the assignment: "Blessed be the LORD, the God of our fathers, who put such a thing as this into the heart of the king, to beautify the house of the LORD that is in Jerusalem, and who extended to me his steadfast love before the king and his counselors. . . . I took courage, for the hand of the LORD my God was on me, and I gathered leading men from Israel to go up with me" (7:27–28).

Yet after Ezra arrives, he is shocked that the Israelites have already broken the Lord's command and married local pagan women (8:1–9:5). It is the kind of sin that brought down God's judgment in Israel's past. Ezra prays for God's mercy:

> O my God, I am ashamed and blush to lift my face to you, my God, for our iniquities have risen higher than our heads. . . . But now for a brief moment favor has been shown by the LORD our God, to leave us a remnant and to give us a secure hold within his holy place, that our God may brighten our eyes and grant

us a little reviving in our slavery. For we are slaves. Yet our God has not forsaken us in our slavery, but has extended to us his steadfast love before the kings of Persia, to grant us some reviving to set up the house of our God, to repair its ruins, and to give us protection in Judea and Jerusalem.

And now, O our God, what shall we say after this? For we have forsaken your commandments. . . . And after all that has come upon us for our evil deeds and for our great guilt, seeing that you, our God, have punished us less than our iniquities deserved and have given us such a remnant as this, *shall we break your commandments again and intermarry with the peoples who practice these abominations? Would you not be angry with us until you consumed us, so that there should be no remnant, nor any to escape?* (9:6–14, emphasis added)

God's entire salvation program for the nations is at stake. So following this heartfelt prayer, Ezra acts, calling on the people to repent and to put away the wives who refuse to follow the Lord (10). Ezra knew something that all God's people have known down through the generations: "Faith apart from works is dead" (James 2:26).

16

Nehemiah 1:11

"O Lord, let your ear be attentive to the prayer of your servant, and to the prayer of your servants who delight to fear your name, and give success to your servant today, and grant him mercy in the sight of this man."
Now I was cupbearer to the king.

THE BOOK OF EZRA TELLS OF THE MORAL BREAKDOWN OF THE returning exiles in Judah. Its sequel, Nehemiah, written by the same author, describes the physical collapse of the walls of Jerusalem. The book also highlights the determined leadership of one man to rebuild—materially and spiritually—for God's glory and the people's good.

Nehemiah, one of the Jewish exiles still living in Babylon a century and a half after the fall of Jerusalem, much like Daniel, has risen to serve King Artaxerxes in the great Persian Empire. It is a position of privilege and responsibility. Yet Nehemiah's heart is with his countrymen who returned to the promised land with Ezra in 458 BC. When, thirteen years later, he hears a distressing report about his beloved Jerusalem, Nehemiah's heart is broken:

> They said to me, "The remnant there in the province who had survived the exile is in great trouble and shame. The wall of Jerusalem is broken down, and its gates are destroyed by fire."

As soon as I heard these words I sat down and wept and
mourned for days, and I continued fasting and praying before
the God of heaven. (1:3–4)

The king's cupbearer throws caution to the wind, requesting
permission from Artaxerxes to rebuild Jerusalem, after his great
prayer of faith: "O Lord, let your ear be attentive to the prayer
of your servant, and to the prayer of your servants who delight
to fear your name, and give success to your servant today, and
grant him mercy in the sight of this man" (1:11). The king grants
his request, setting in motion a pattern for Nehemiah of seeing a
need, praying about it, and acting in faith (2:4–5; 4:1–9).

In answering Nehemiah's prayer, the Lord enables his servant
to rebuild the walls of Jerusalem in only fifty-two days (2:1–6:15),
deal with oppression of the poor by fellow Jews (5:1–13), encourage a repentant people when the Law is read by Ezra (8:9–12), eject
foreign enemies from the temple (13:1–9), and establish proper
temple worship (13:30–31).

And Nehemiah does all this despite constant opposition and at
great personal cost. Sanballat the Horonite, whom the Elephantine
papyri later identify as governor of Samaria,[1] and Tobiah the
Ammonite are "displeased . . . greatly that someone had come to
seek the welfare of the people of Israel" (2:10). Later joined by
Geshem the Arab, they allege that Nehemiah is plotting rebellion
against the king (2:19). They jeer at and threaten those rebuilding
the wall (4:1–12). Nehemiah responds with exhortation, prayer,
and preparation (4:13–23). The workers are both armed and
guarded. When Israel's enemies seek to lure Nehemiah from the
work, he is immovable (6:1–14).

Not only does Nehemiah oppose usury, he serves as a shin-
ing example of integrity (5:14–19). For twelve years, neither he as
governor nor his associates eat at public expense "because of the

fear of God" (5:15). He works on the wall with his servants, buys no land, and pays for his group's considerable provisions. It is an illustration of Christ's words: "Whoever would be great among you must be your servant, and whoever would be first among you must be slave of all" (Mark 10:43–44).

"Remember for my good, O my God," Nehemiah prays, "all that I have done for this people" (5:19). It is a prayer that no doubt was answered. "For truly, I say to you," Jesus said, "whoever gives you a cup of water to drink because you belong to Christ will by no means lose his reward" (Mark 9:41).

The people, like many of the Lord's followers before and after, are a difficult bunch to govern. Though they return wholeheartedly to the Lord and set up temple worship according to Nehemiah's instructions (8–12), they allow pagan Tobiah a foothold in the temple. The temple administration is in shambles. The people are breaking the Sabbath and even marrying foreign women again (13:1–24). So Nehemiah, who had gone back to Babylon to serve Artaxerxes, returns by the mercy of the pagan king to set things right once more (13:6–7; 11–22; 25–28).

With the wall rebuilt, the temple reorganized, and the people set on the right path by their godly servant leader, the Lord's calling on Israel to be a light to the nations can continue. His success finally assured, Nehemiah asks for the Lord's blessings a last time: "Remember me, O my God, for good" (13:31). Nehemiah knows that the Lord who moves in world history can also be trusted to bless his followers' lives.

17

Esther 4:14

If you keep silent at this time, relief and deliverance will rise for the Jews from another place, but you and your father's house will perish. And who knows whether you have not come to the kingdom for such a time as this?

ESTHER, THOUGH PRESENTED AFTER EZRA AND NEHEMIAH IN OUR English Bibles, actually depicts events in the reign of the Persian king Ahasuerus (Xerxes I) from 486 to 464 BC, about midway between the proclamation of Cyrus and the ministries of Ezra and Nehemiah. According to the Jewish historian Josephus, Esther was the last book written in the Jewish canon,[1] which explains its placement as the final of the Old Testament's historical books.

The story opens with drunken royal feasting in Susa and a bitter parting of the ways between Xerxes and Queen Vashti (1). The king approves of a plan to replace her as queen. "Beautiful young virgins" from across the empire are brought in (2:1–4).

Among them is a Jewish woman named Hadassah (Persian name Esther). She is being raised by Mordecai, her uncle, descendant of exiles from Jerusalem in 597. Esther is prepared to meet Xerxes, who does not know she is a Jew. Against all odds, the Jewish girl pleases him and is named queen (2:5–18).

In the book, God is not mentioned or seen, but his sovereign and loving presence on behalf of his people is written on every page. Time after time, events in the faraway empire come together providentially to protect the Jews, who would otherwise be at the mercy of their pagan enemies.

With Esther's help, Mordecai quickly shows his value to the earthly kingdom, foiling a plot against Xerxes (2:19–23). But as a citizen of God's kingdom, he refuses to bow to Haman, a descendant of the Amalekites, enemies of the Jews (Ex. 17; 1 Sam. 15).[2] Enraged, Haman launches his own plot—to exterminate the Jewish people (3).

Mordecai asks Esther to use her access to the king to "plead with him on behalf of her people" (4:8). Esther, fearing possible execution (and knowing that Xerxes is ignorant of her Jewish heritage), hesitates. So in the key verse Mordecai warns his niece: "If you keep silent at this time, relief and deliverance will rise for the Jews from another place, but you and your father's house will perish. And who knows whether you have not come to the kingdom for such a time as this?" (4:14).

Mordecai trusts in the hidden Lord's presence and power, but he also knows that God's people are responsible to play their own roles in the divine drama. Esther understands and agrees to go to the king. Then she adds, "If I perish, I perish" (4:16). She invites Xerxes and Haman to a banquet, offering a second feast the next day (5:1–8). Haman goes home flattered, only to be enraged again by Mordecai. Haman's wife and friends suggest that a gallows seventy-five feet high be built for Mordecai before Haman goes to Esther's second feast (5:9–14). Anti-Semitism runs deep in the Persian Empire apparently.

That night, however, a sleepless Xerxes learns from the royal archives about Mordecai's earlier service (6:1–3). Then enters Haman, full of himself. The king asks him, "What should be done to the man whom the king delights to honor?" Proud Haman, thinking *he* is the man, replies, "Let royal robes be brought . . . and the horse that the king has ridden, and . . . a royal crown. . . . And let . . . the king's most noble officials, . . . dress the man whom the king delights to honor, and let them lead him on the horse through the square of the city, proclaiming . . . : 'Thus shall it be done to the man whom the king delights to honor'" (6:6–9).

Then comes the devastating royal reply: "Hurry; take the robes and the horse, as you have said, and do so to Mordecai the Jew" (6:10). Haman is forced to publicly honor Mordecai, whom he hates, and his alarmed wife and counselors prophesy, "You . . . will surely fall before him" (6:13).

Next, like a steer being led to slaughter, Haman is hustled off to Esther's second feast (7), where Esther reveals the aim of "wicked Haman" (7:6). Seeking mercy, he falls on the queen's couch, and the king, enraged once more, interprets this as attempted assault. Xerxes pronounces judgment: Haman will be hanged on the gallows he himself built for Mordecai (7:10).

Moreover, God's people throughout the empire receive permission to defend themselves against the earlier edict (8) and set their enemies to flight (9:1–19). The Jews' lament turns to rejoicing, launching the festival of Purim (9:20–32). Mordecai, in God's sovereign orchestration of history, is raised to Haman's position (10).

The book is full of reversals, ironies, humor, and hatred. Through it all, God delivers his people who, like Esther, participate responsibly in the divine plan.

18

Job 42:6

I despise myself,
and repent in dust and ashes.

"THERE WAS A MAN IN THE LAND OF UZ WHOSE NAME WAS JOB," the book that bears his name begins, "and that man was blameless and upright, one who feared God and turned away from evil" (1:1). Yet Job, a man of great wealth, is about to lose everything.

The scene suddenly shifts to the heavenly throne room, where angelic beings and Satan stand before the Lord (1:6–12). God initiates a dialogue with the fallen angel (Rev. 12:4), who says he has been out canvassing the earth. The Lord points out righteous Job to the Devil, who sneers, "Stretch out your hand and touch all that he has, and he will curse you to your face" (Job 1:11). God then permits Satan to test Job's faith and character.

The calamities come in quick succession (1:13–20): Job loses his livestock, servants, and children. But his response is remarkable: "Naked I came from my mother's womb, and naked shall I return. The LORD gave, and the LORD has taken away; blessed be the name of the LORD" (1:21). The author adds in seeming wonderment, "In all this Job did not sin or charge God with wrong" (1:22).

Seeing Job's reaction, Satan changes his tack before the Lord: "Stretch out your hand and touch his bone and his flesh, and he will curse you to your face" (2:5). The Lord allows this trial, too, and Job gets "loathsome sores from the sole of his foot to the crown of his head" (2:7). At this point, his grieving wife, apparently speaking for the Devil, says, "Do you still hold fast your integrity? Curse God and die" (2:9). And yet, "in all this Job did not sin with his lips" (2:10).

Then we come to the poetic heart of the book, the three friends who come to comfort Job (2:11–31:40): Eliphaz the Temanite, Bildad the Shuhite, and Zophar the Naamathite. They start well, sitting with him on the ground for seven full days, "and no one spoke a word to him, for they saw that his suffering was very great" (2:13).

Job finally cries out, "Why did I not die at birth . . . ?" (3:11). Then the three friends attempt to prove to suffering Job that God always grants prosperity to the righteous and punishes the wicked (4:1–25:6). They imply—or say outright—that Job has done something to deserve his fate. The reader knows better.

This poetic section consists of three cycles of dialogue between the friends and Job (4:1–14:22; 15:1–21:34; 22:1–25:6)—with the third ending early, the four men apparently at an impasse. Throughout, an increasingly bitter Job insists on his integrity and asks that God appear and explain himself. Atheism is not an option, however. "I know that my Redeemer lives," he says, "and at the last he will stand upon the earth" (19:25).

After Job makes a final plea for vindication (26–31), another character—Elihu—appears to defend God's honor, reprove the friends and Job, and commend the value of suffering in a person's life (32–37).

After all this talk by the humans, the Lord finally *does* appear (38:1–42:6). But rather than justify his actions or reveal his wager with Satan, God offers two bracing catalogs of his wisdom and might in the created order. "Where were you when I laid the foundation of the earth?" he asks a suddenly silent Job from out of the whirlwind. "Tell me, if you have understanding" (38:4). Job, of course, was nowhere and has none.

Seeing the Lord's majesty and realizing his own utter ignorance and empty words, Job replies meekly, "I despise myself, / and repent in dust and ashes" (42:6). Trust is the turning point for Job and for all who suffer and don't know why. Having seen the power and wisdom of his Creator, Job no longer needs an answer for his predicament. He has seen God, and that is enough.

The Lord, however, is not finished. Job is to pray for his three friends, "for [they] have not spoken of me what is right, as my servant Job has" (42:7). Despite Job's anger and frustration, the Lord accepts him and blesses "the latter days of Job more than his beginning" (42:12).

Like Job, most faithful believers in the Lord learn that our suffering is not erased but redeemed—in this life or the next. As Jesus said, "Everyone who has left houses or brothers or sisters or father or mother or children or lands, for my name's sake, will receive a hundredfold and will inherit eternal life" (Matt. 19:29).

19

Psalm 16:11

You make known to me the path of life;
in your presence there is fullness of joy;
at your right hand are pleasures forevermore.

MARTIN LUTHER CALLED THE BOOK OF PSALMS "THE BIBLE IN miniature."[1] This book of worship for God's people seeks to orient us to a joyful, God-focused life. God, the key verse tells us, loves his children, knows what we need, and offers us "fullness of joy" from his inexhaustible supplies both now and forever.

The psalms, as outstanding examples of Hebrew poetry, exhibit the following literary features in varying measures, according to Bible scholar Walter Elwell:[2]

Word structure. Each line contains two to four words, each of which is accented, forming a meter. The most common meter has three words (or word units) in the first line and three in the second, forming a 3+3 meter. Others are 2+2, 3+2, and 3+3+3.

Parallelism. A repetition of thought, not of sound. The basic unit is a balanced couplet, with pauses at the middle and end.

Acrostic. Each verse in an acrostic psalm begins with a successive letter of the twenty-two-letter Hebrew alphabet (Pss. 9; 10; 25; 34; 37; 111; 112; 145). The lengthy Psalm 119, meanwhile, features twenty-two eight-verse sections, each of which begins with a different Hebrew letter.

Though the Psalter is one book, Elwell divides it into the following categories, which reflect the full range of human experience and need:[3]

Praise. "The Hebrew title, 'Praises,' defines accurately a large part of the contents of the book," Elwell notes. "Each of the first four sections concludes with a doxology, while the fifth section concludes with five psalms, each of which begins or ends with one or two 'Hallelujahs.'"

Examples: Psalms 9; 29; 47; 103; 124

Zion. "Praise of Zion," Elwell says, "was, in fact, almost synonymous with praise of the Lord who dwelt there. Jerusalem's continued survival, in spite of its vicissitudes, was ample demonstration of God's enduring greatness . . . and peculiar affection for the city which housed his temple."

Examples: Psalms 48; 76; 84; 87; 122

Laments. Though we are called to a life of worship, praise, and joy, the Psalms are realistic. Suffering is no strange thing. There are two main kinds of lament in the Psalms—*national* (because of drought, war, and so on; Pss. 14; 44; 60), and *individual* (Pss. 13; 22). Psalms of individual lament constitute "the backbone of the psalter" and frequently conclude with praise to God. There are fifty individual lament psalms, which can be further subdivided into *imprecatory* (Ps. 109), *passion* (Ps. 16), and *penitential* (Ps. 32).

Wisdom. Reflecting the approach of Job, Proverbs, and Ecclesiastes, wisdom in the Psalms involves both knowing and doing the right thing, based upon God's law, involving one's intellect and ethics.

Examples: Psalms 1; 37; 49; 73; 127; 128

The Davidic King. The royal psalms refer to the king, his rule, and his relationship to the Lord. They ultimately point beyond Israel's earthly kings, who ruled for fewer than five hundred years, to a coming messianic King.

Examples: Psalms 2; 18; 20; 21; 45; 61; 72; 89; 101; 110; 132; 144

Whatever the subject and structure of the Psalms, the life of joy runs through the book like a mountain stream. The one who trusts in the Lord

> *. . . is like a tree*
> *planted by streams of water*
> *that yields its fruit in its season,*
> *and its leaf does not wither.*
> *In all that he does, he prospers.* (Ps. 1:3)

This life of joy finds its ultimate expression in the ministry of Jesus Christ and the filling of the Holy Spirit. As the Lord said, "If anyone thirsts, let him come to me and drink. Whoever believes in me, as the Scripture has said, 'Out of his heart will flow rivers of living water'" (John 7:37–38).

20

Proverbs 1:7

The fear of the LORD is the beginning of knowledge;
fools despise wisdom and instruction.

PROVERBS PROVIDES A RICH SAMPLING OF THE THREE THOUSAND short, pithy sayings attributed to King Solomon, among other features. The book's subject, broadly speaking, is wisdom, but not just *any* wisdom. Mark Dever says that "it is not simply a book of secular proverbs, like 'Early to bed, early to rise, makes a man healthy, wealthy, and wise.'"[1] Going to bed and rising early provide no *guarantee* of success, but doing both is usually a good idea. Biblical proverbs, like their secular counterparts, tell what *generally* happens when we follow their principles in God's sin-scarred world. These are proverbs, not promises.

The key verse, 1:7, sets the tone. The foundation of knowledge (or wisdom, according to 9:10) is not intelligence or education but "the fear of the LORD." Those who love God in reverent fear have a huge advantage over others. Anyone can accumulate facts. Some, like Einstein and Newton, can propose theories. But only those who put God first can understand what life is all about and live in that light.

The verse contrasts people who acquire godly knowledge with "fools [who] despise wisdom and instruction." Being a fool, biblically speaking, is a moral status even more than an intellectual failing. Much of the rest of Proverbs fleshes out this contrast between the wise and the foolish, as Jesus juxtaposed the wise and foolish builders (Matt. 7:24–27) and the wise and foolish virgins (Matt. 25:1–13).

One group is on the road to life; the other to death. "Enter by the narrow gate," Jesus said. "For the gate is wide and the way is easy that leads to destruction, and those who enter by it are many. For the gate is narrow and the way is hard that leads to life, and those who find it are few" (Matt. 7:13–14).

In the first section (Prov. 1:8–9:18), we have a father's teaching to his son to acquire wisdom, which is sometimes personified as a woman:

> *Wisdom cries aloud in the street,*
> *in the markets she raises her voice; . . .*
> *"If you turn at my reproof,*
> *behold, I will pour out my spirit to you;*
> *I will make my words known to you.*
> *Because I have called and you refused to listen,*
> *have stretched out my hand and no one has heeded,*
> *because you have ignored all my counsel*
> *and would have none of my reproof,*
> *I also will laugh at your calamity;*
> *I will mock when terror strikes you,*
> *when terror strikes you like a storm*
> *and your calamity comes like a whirlwind,*
> *when distress and anguish come upon you." (1:20–27)*

The section, composed of several short poems, warns against greed, illicit sex, laziness, and robbery, and encourages the fear of God, according to Lady Wisdom:

> *For whoever finds me finds life*
> *and obtains favor from the* Lord,
> *but he who fails to find me injures himself;*
> *all who hate me love death. (8:35–36)*

The book's next section (10:1–22:16) is titled "The Proverbs of Solomon." It consists mostly of brief statements, sometimes grouped together by theme, on honesty, diligence, and discretion—or their opposites. As with the first section, we are meant to learn from and please our parents. Here is a brief selection from chapter 11:

> *Riches do not profit in the day of wrath,*
> *but righteousness delivers from death. (v. 4)*

> *When it goes well with the righteous, the city rejoices,*
> *and when the wicked perish there are shouts of gladness.*
> *(v. 10)*

> *Where there is no guidance, a people falls,*
> *but in an abundance of counselors there is safety. (v. 14)*

> *The wicked earns deceptive wages,*
> *but one who sows righteousness gets a sure reward. (v. 18)*

> *One gives freely, yet grows all the richer;*
> *another withholds what he should give, and only suffers want.*
> *Whoever brings blessing will be enriched,*
> *and one who waters will himself be watered. (vv. 24–25)*

The next sections collect sayings of "the Wise" (22:17–24:34), Solomon again (from King Hezekiah, 25–29), Agur (30), and King Lemuel (31:1–9). The book ends with the portrait of a godly wife and mother (31:10–31):

> *Strength and dignity are her clothing,*
> *and she laughs at the time to come.*
> *She opens her mouth with wisdom,*
> *and the teaching of kindness is on her tongue.*
> *She looks well to the ways of her household*
> *and does not eat the bread of idleness.*
> *Her children rise up and call her blessed;*
> *her husband also, and he praises her:*
> *"Many women have done excellently,*
> *but you surpass them all."*
> *Charm is deceitful, and beauty is vain,*
> *but a woman who fears the* LORD *is to be praised.*
> *Give her of the fruit of her hands,*
> *and let her works praise her in the gates. (31:25–31)*

As with the rest of Proverbs, the blessings of wisdom in this woman's life are obvious and worth emulating.

21

Ecclesiastes 1:3

What does man gain by all the toil
at which he toils under the sun?

FOR ANYONE TEMPTED TO THINK THAT PROVERBS IS A SIMPLE ROAD map to success in this life and the next, there is Ecclesiastes to show that success is not all that it is cracked up to be. "If . . . Proverbs is about wisdom for people who *want* success, . . . Ecclesiastes offers wisdom for people who have success," says Mark Dever. "Particularly, it is for individuals who have gotten what they wanted out of life, or at least what they *thought* they had wanted, and then have found it wanting."[1]

Written by a man who calls himself "the Preacher" (1:1), Ecclesiastes begins with a seeming cry of despair: "Vanity of vanities, says the Preacher, / vanity of vanities! All is vanity" (1:2).

The Hebrew word translated by the English Standard Version as "vanity" is HEBEL (literally, vapor). Other translators have rendered the word, which appears thirty-four times in the book, as "meaningless" (NIV) or even "enigmatic."[2] The point seems to be that nothing lasts in this world, and there is no way to figure out why. Certainly our key verse (1:3) highlights the transience of our work and existence: "What does man gain by all the toil / at which he toils under the sun?"

Human beings are not animals. Even if we fulfill all our needs for food, shelter, physical intimacy, and achievement, we need more. We want meaning and significance, the Preacher says, but we cannot obtain them in this life—or at least we cannot *keep* them. The seeming randomness of life keeps us humble. It is a shock to realize that human wisdom can take us only so far.

"I applied my heart to seek and to search out by wisdom all that is done under heaven," says the Preacher (who may or may not be King Solomon). "It is an unhappy business that God has given to the children of man to be busy with. I have seen everything that is done under the sun, and behold, all is vanity and a striving after wind" (1:13–14).

Much of the book is a dreary but gripping catalog of the author's futile attempts to discover meaning in everything "under the sun" and finding none. Unlike most humans who have walked the planet, he has the opportunity and the inclination to do it all. First, he tests pleasure, everything from laughter, to alcohol, to materialism, to sex (2:1–11). All, however, are found to be "vanity and a striving after wind, and there was nothing to be gained under the sun" (2:11). Then he sees that a wise life cannot protect from death (2:12–17) and work cannot bring peace (2:18–23).

But what comes next (2:24–25) injects the book's first note of hope. "There is nothing better for a person than that he should eat and drink and find enjoyment in his toil," the Preacher says. "This also, I saw, is from the hand of God, for apart from him who can eat or who can have enjoyment?" While we cannot find ultimate meaning in the things of this world, we are not to despise them. Instead, we should gratefully accept them as blessings from the hand of God, who stands outside our wearisome lives "under the sun."

Cultivating joy amid an uncertain existence is a theme that pops up throughout Ecclesiastes, just when the clouds of doubt are darkest (3:12–13; 5:18–19; 8:15; 9:7). We don't have to grasp all the answers to enjoy life as God's gift in the here and now.

That's a good perspective when time seems to wind on without purpose (3:1–15), injustice and oppression reign (3:16–4:3), and human sin and dysfunction cloud our days (4:4–16). Like the sun that ceaselessly rises and sets (1:5) and the wind that ever sighs along the same pathways (1:6), there seems to be no direction to life, no destination. Yet despite all the uncertainty, worship of the true God gives us an anchor for the soul (5), even when we are blown about by the vanity of politics, injustice, death as the great leveler, and even human moderation (6:1–11:6).

What is the point of all our labor "under the sun"? The Preacher points us again and again to God, who will one day be our Judge (11:9; 12:1, 7, 14). "The end of the matter," we are told, is to "fear God and keep his commandments, for this is the whole duty of man" (12:13).

This statement is a precursor to Paul's even greater encouragement for Christians: "My beloved brothers, be steadfast, immovable, always abounding in the work of the Lord, knowing that in the Lord your labor is not in vain" (1 Cor. 15:58). Our lives and everything in them matter because they matter to our Creator and Redeemer.

22

Song of Songs 6:3

*I am my beloved's and my beloved is mine;
he grazes among the lilies.*

THE SONG OF SONGS (OR SONG OF SOLOMON) DECISIVELY REFUTES the old lie that biblical faith is antisex. The last of the Bible's five books of Wisdom Literature, the Song celebrates marital intimacy while pointing God's people to the ultimate consummation between their heavenly Bridegroom and his bride.

Questions abound concerning the author and structure of the book. Some interpreters see Solomon as the author (Song 1:1; 1 Kings 4:32). Others say that the book was written in his honor and that the events of Solomon's life don't seem to match what the Song portrays (1 Kings 2:46). Still others say the book is a collection of love poems.[1]

One need not commit to a single interpretation of these matters to recognize the main point of the Song. Our key verse describes the self-giving intention of all true lovers, an echo of the bliss of Adam, who said with delight when he saw Eve for the first time: "This at last is bone of my bones / and flesh of my flesh" (Gen. 2:23).

The images of love and sexual desire presented throughout the Song are, to modern ears, both familiar and strange—familiar in that they describe near universal human longings, but strange in that they employ ancient Near Eastern metaphors and similes that occasionally sound jarring to twenty-first-century ears:

> *I compare you, my love,*
> > *to a mare among Pharaoh's chariots. (1:9)*

> *Behold, you are beautiful, my love,*
> > *behold, you are beautiful!*
> *Your eyes are doves*
> > *behind your veil.*
> *Your hair is like a flock of goats*
> > *leaping down the slopes of Gilead.*
> *Your teeth are like a flock of shorn ewes*
> > *that have come up from the washing,*
> *all of which bear twins,*
> > *and not one among them has lost its young.*
> *Your lips are like a scarlet thread,*
> > *and your mouth is lovely.*
> *Your cheeks are like halves of a pomegranate*
> > *behind your veil.*
> *Your neck is like the tower of David,*
> > *built in rows of stone;*
> *on it hang a thousand shields,*
> > *all of them shields of warriors. (4:1–4)*

Yet the strangeness soon gives way to language with uncomfortably clear meaning for those unaccustomed to the Bible's frankness about sexual desire:

> *Your two breasts are like two fawns,*
> > *twins of a gazelle,*
> > *that graze among the lilies. . . .*

You are altogether beautiful, my love;
    there is no flaw in you....
You have captivated my heart, my sister, my bride;
    you have captivated my heart with one glance of your eyes,
    with one jewel of your necklace.
How beautiful is your love, my sister, my bride!
    How much better is your love than wine,
    and the fragrance of your oils than any spice!
Your lips drip nectar, my bride;
    honey and milk are under your tongue;
    the fragrance of your garments is like the fragrance
    of Lebanon. (4:5–11)

In contrast to the ancient (and sometimes modern) view of women as mere property or playthings of men, the Song portrays the woman as a full partner in the divinely sanctioned romance. She shares her lover's excitement about what is to come, not as an object to be exploited, but as a fellow bearer of the divine image anticipating and enjoying the Lord's good gift of physical, emotional, and spiritual union:

> *If I found you outside, I would kiss you,*
>   *and none would despise me....*
> *His left hand is under my head,*
>   *and his right hand embraces me! (8:1–3)*

The woman, bold in her love and sense of belonging, calls on the man to be a faithful husband that they might truly belong to each other (6:3):

> *Set me as a seal upon your heart,*
>   *as a seal upon your arm,*

for love is strong as death,
jealousy is fierce as the grave.
Its flashes are flashes of fire,
the very flame of the LORD.
Many waters cannot quench love,
neither can floods drown it.
If a man offered for love
all the wealth of his house,
he would be utterly despised. (8:6–7)

The Song provides a picture of human love and longing that Christians can't help noticing is an anticipation of Jesus Christ, who "loved the church and gave himself up for her, that he might sanctify her, having cleansed her by the washing of water with the word, so that he might present the church to himself in splendor, without spot or wrinkle or any such thing, that she might be holy and without blemish" (Eph. 5:25–27).

23

Isaiah 40:9

Go on up to a high mountain,
O Zion, herald of good news;
lift up your voice with strength,
O Jerusalem, herald of good news;
lift it up, fear not;
say to the cities of Judah,
"Behold your God!"

THOUGH NOT EVERY BOOK IN THE BIBLE MENTIONS GOD,[1] EACH, like the facet of a diamond, distinctively shows forth the Lord's faithful dealings with the world and his people. But the book of Isaiah presents such an incomparable portrait of the Sovereign of the universe that the climax of our key verse—"Behold your God!"—seems inescapable.

Isaiah, the first of the prophetic books in our Bibles, was written between 740 and 680 BC, a momentous era encompassing the decline and fall of the Northern Kingdom and the spiritual declension of Judah. Isaiah was likely a southerner (1:1) who called God's people to return to their divinely given role to model God's goodness and holiness before the nations.

The prophet's concerns, however, ranged far beyond the immediate circumstances of Israel and Judah, covering the coming exile of Judah by Babylon, the people's predicted return under

Cyrus of Persia, the promised Messiah who would die for his people, and visions of a world ultimately set right. In all, we see a God who sovereignly cares for his undeserving but needy people, bringing them good news for today and throughout eternity. Rightly beholding this God enables his people to grow in faith, whatever circumstances life throws at them.

The book starts with a summary of the sins of Judah (1–5), home to the temple, where God dwells in a special way with his people. Despite all their privileges, the people are described as a "sinful nation . . . laden with iniquity . . . offspring of evildoers . . . children who deal corruptly" (1:4). From a human perspective, all seems to be falling apart.

Then Isaiah receives his call as a prophet:

> In the year that King Uzziah died I saw the Lord sitting upon a throne, high and lifted up; and the train of his robe filled the temple. Above him stood the seraphim. Each had six wings: with two he covered his face, and with two he covered his feet, and with two he flew. And one called to another and said:
>
> > "Holy, holy, holy is the LORD of hosts;
> > the whole earth is full of his glory!"
>
> And the foundations of the thresholds shook at the voice of him who called, and the house was filled with smoke. And I said: "Woe is me! For I am lost; for I am a man of unclean lips, and I dwell in the midst of a people of unclean lips; for my eyes have seen the King, the LORD of hosts!" (6:1–5)

Isaiah has beheld his holy and omnipotent God, and he spends the rest of his life sharing that vision with tiny, insecure Judah.

This is a God who rules over his people (7:1–12:6) and the nations (13:1–35:10). We see his mighty care for Jerusalem in miraculously thwarting the blasphemous attack of Sennacherib (36–37), who considers the Lord as just another national god. Godly King Hezekiah then has a personal deliverance from God (38) before he stumbles, setting in motion Judah's ultimate destruction at the hands of Babylon (39).

The scene suddenly shifts in chapters 40–55. Isaiah is looking ahead to the Lord's future deliverance of the exiles from among the nations. This God is not like the pagan gods. He is both mighty (40:10) and loving (40:11). The people, fainting from their long exile, can trust him as they behold his saving acts:

> Have you not known? Have you not heard?
> The LORD is the everlasting God,
>   the Creator of the ends of the earth.
> He does not faint or grow weary;
>   his understanding is unsearchable.
> He gives power to the faint,
>   and to him who has no might he increases strength.
>   (40:28–29)

Throughout the book, Isaiah speaks of a coming One called "Mighty God" and "Prince of Peace" (9:6). This Prince is in Jesse's line, with the Spirit resting on him, a righteous judge who will inaugurate universal peace (11:1–10). Not only this, he carries the people's sorrows and is punished for their sins (53:1–9). Yet the Lord will raise this Servant back to life (53:10–12). It is a dizzying vision of God's Messiah, who indeed is God himself.

The book closes (56–66) with a call for the people to get ready to meet this God, who will fully restore Israel (60) and renew heaven and earth:

The sun shall be no more
  your light by day,
nor for brightness shall the moon
  give you light;
*but the L*ORD *will be your everlasting light,*
  and your God will be your glory. (60:19)

After being expelled from Eden, all God's people shall finally behold God again . . . face-to-face (Rev. 21:3).

24

Jeremiah 31:33

This is the covenant that I will make with the house of
Israel after those days, declares the LORD: I will put my
law within them, and I will write it on their hearts. And
I will be their God, and they shall be my people.

JEREMIAH HAS BEEN CALLED THE "WEEPING PROPHET,"[1] AND NOT
without reason. Ministering about a century after Isaiah, who
saw God's miraculous deliverance of Jerusalem, Jeremiah fore-
sees God's judgment on a wayward people, who have forsaken
the covenant. Speaking for God, who sounds like a jilted lover,
Jeremiah says,

> *What wrong did your fathers find in me*
> *that they went far from me,*
> *and went after worthlessness, and became worthless? ...*
>
> *Has a nation changed its gods,*
> *even though they are no gods?*
> *But my people have changed their glory*
> *for that which does not profit.*
> *Be appalled, O heavens, at this;*
> *be shocked, be utterly desolate,*
> *declares the LORD,*

for my people have committed two evils:
they have forsaken me,
*   the fountain of living waters,*
and hewed out cisterns for themselves,
*   broken cisterns that can hold no water. (2:5, 11–13)*

The judgment that the Lord promises will be severe:

Flee for safety, O people of Benjamin,
*   from the midst of Jerusalem!*
Blow the trumpet in Tekoa,
*   and raise a signal on Beth-haccherem,*
for disaster looms out of the north,
*   and great destruction.*
The lovely and delicately bred I will destroy,
*   the daughter of Zion. . . .*

For thus says the LORD of hosts:
"Cut down her trees;
*   cast up a siege mound against Jerusalem.*
This is the city that must be punished;
*   there is nothing but oppression within her." (6:1–2, 6)*

Though the Lord spared the people from Assyria, he will not protect them from Babylon. Judah's time of spiritual prostitution is over. God's punishment looms. The city where sacrifices are offered to God is doomed. It is a horrifying message that wins Jeremiah plenty of enemies. Yet the Lord assures his prophet of his calling:

Before I formed you in the womb I knew you,
*   and before you were born I consecrated you;*
I appointed you a prophet to the nations. (1:5)

Jeremiah replies timidly, "Ah, Lord GOD! Behold, I do not know how to speak, for I am only a youth" (1:6). So the Lord reassures him:

> Do not say, "I am only a youth";
> for to all to whom I send you, you shall go,
> and whatever I command you, you shall speak.
> Do not be afraid of them,
> for I am with you to deliver you,
> declares the LORD. (1:7–8)

Yet the path that the Lord has chosen for Jeremiah and walks with him is anything but easy. Jeremiah suffers even as he bears God's message of impending judgment on Israel (1–45) and on Babylon (46–51). "I am full of the wrath of the LORD," he says; "I am weary of holding it in" (6:11).

In his long years as a "prophet to the nations," Jeremiah sees only two converts: Baruch, his scribe; and Ebed-melech, an Ethiopian eunuch.[2] Jeremiah is thrown into a dungeon by Zedekiah (37), the last king of Judah, and eventually exiled in Egypt, where some fellow Jews forcibly take him after the fall of Jerusalem in 586 BC (43).

However, amid all the condemnation, God reminds the unfaithful people that he will remain faithful. Jeremiah sends a group of exiles in Babylon a letter from God telling them the captivity is only temporary. "I know the plans I have for you," the letter promises, ". . . plans for welfare and not for evil, to give you a future and a hope. Then you will call upon me and come and pray to me, and I will hear you. You will seek me and find me, when you seek me with all your heart" (29:11–13). It is a breathtaking statement of grace.

Then Jeremiah shares an even more astounding prophecy— the unilateral promise of a coming "new covenant" (31:31). The people have failed in their covenant obligations, so the Lord will give them a fresh start. More than that, he will enable them to finally keep this covenant from the heart: "For this is the covenant that I will make with the house of Israel after those days, declares the LORD: I will put my law within them, and I will write it on their hearts. And I will be their God, and they shall be my people" (31:33).

This covenant would come via the perfect sacrifice of Jesus Christ, who "entered once for all into the holy places, not by means of the blood of goats and calves but by means of his own blood, thus securing an eternal redemption" (Heb. 9:12).

25

Lamentations 3:22

The steadfast love of the LORD never ceases;
his mercies never come to an end.

WHAT DO YOU DO WHEN THE WORST THING THAT COULD CONCEIVABLY happen actually happens? For the believer in God, of course, the answer is to trust in the Lord. Yes, but is that all? Not if Lamentations is to be taken seriously. First you lament.

Written shortly after the fall of Jerusalem in 586 BC, the book is actually five poems, "a collection of laments, or melancholy dirges, for a ruined society."[1] Each dirge is a chapter in the book. Yet they are dirges with a difference. The first four are written as acrostics, each beginning with a successive letter of the twenty-two-character Hebrew alphabet, from *aleph* to *taw*.

The exception in this group, both structurally and thematically, is chapter 3, which has three times as many verses and which presents an acrostic in groups of three letters. The first three verses begin with *aleph*, the next three with *beth*, and so on. Commentators believe this careful structure in part reflects a desire for order amid all the chaos.

Lamentations begins by describing Jerusalem's fall in the starkest terms:

How lonely sits the city
    that was full of people!
How like a widow has she become,
    she who was great among the nations!
She who was a princess among the provinces
    has become a slave.

She weeps bitterly in the night,
    with tears on her cheeks;
among all her lovers
    she has none to comfort her;
all her friends have dealt treacherously with her;
    they have become her enemies.

Judah has gone into exile because of affliction
    and hard servitude;
she dwells now among the nations,
    but finds no resting place;
her pursuers have all overtaken her
    in the midst of her distress. (1:1–3)

The images are shocking, at least to those who are unaccustomed to the dark side of life or who wonder how God could allow such things to happen, especially to his people. They are disturbing to the author of Lamentations (perhaps Jeremiah) as well:

My eyes are spent with weeping;
    my stomach churns;
my bile is poured out to the ground
    because of the destruction of the daughter of my people,
because infants and babies faint
    in the streets of the city. . . .

Should women eat the fruit of their womb,
  the children of their tender care?
Should priest and prophet be killed
  in the sanctuary of the Lord? (2:11, 20)

Amid all the suffering, we see a persistent and growing recognition that Israel has sinned and has gotten what it deserved: "Jerusalem sinned grievously" (1:8); "My transgressions were bound into a yoke" (1:14); "The LORD is in the right, / for I have rebelled against his word" (1:18); "I have been very rebellious" (1:20); and "The LORD has done what he purposed" (2:17).

Chapter 3, the spiritual summit of Lamentations, takes this recognition to a new level, transforming it into trust:

Remember my affliction and my wanderings,
  the wormwood and the gall!
My soul continually remembers it
  and is bowed down within me.
But this I call to mind,
  and therefore I have hope:

The steadfast love of the LORD never ceases;
  his mercies never come to an end;
they are new every morning;
  great is your faithfulness.
"The LORD is my portion," says my soul,
  "therefore I will hope in him." (3:19–24)

Such individual trust is based on God's covenantal "steadfast love" in the past and our faith in what he has promised for the future. Therefore, God's children can endure any suffering, even the self-inflicted kind. The Lord is our portion, now and forever.

The book concludes with further expressions of suffering (4), which does not always end when we exercise faith, and the community's prayer for restoration (5). It is a realistic plea, not at all Pollyannaish:

> *Women are raped in Zion,*
>   *young women in the towns of Judah.*
> *Princes are hung up by their hands;*
>   *no respect is shown to the elders....*
> *The crown has fallen from our head;*
>   *woe to us, for we have sinned!*
> *For this our heart has become sick,*
>   *for these things our eyes have grown dim,*
> *for Mount Zion which lies desolate;*
>   *jackals prowl over it.*
> *But you, O LORD, reign forever;*
>   *your throne endures to all generations.*
> *Why do you forget us forever,*
>   *why do you forsake us for so many days?*
> *Restore us to yourself, O LORD, that we may be restored!*
>   *(5:11–12, 16–21)*

Pointing to the Lord's steadfast love, Lamentations gives us permission to be honest with God and with ourselves.

26

Ezekiel 36:22

Say to the house of Israel, Thus says the Lord GOD: It is not for your sake, O house of Israel, that I am about to act, but for the sake of my holy name, which you have profaned among the nations to which you came.

A YOUNG EZEKIEL IS SENT INTO EXILE IN BABYLON WITH SEV-eral thousand of Judah's finest, about a decade before Nebuchadnezzar's army levels Jerusalem. Five years before that fateful day, however, Ezekiel, in the priestly line, receives a vision—the first of many in his long apocalyptic masterpiece:

As I looked, behold, a stormy wind came out of the north, and a great cloud, with brightness around it, and fire flashing forth continually, and in the midst of the fire, as it were gleam-ing metal. And from the midst of it came the likeness of four living creatures. And this was their appearance: they had a human likeness, but each had four faces, and each of them had four wings. Their legs were straight, and the soles of their feet were like the sole of a calf's foot. And they sparkled like burnished bronze. Under their wings on their four sides they had human hands. . . . Each creature had two wings, each of which touched the wing of another, while two covered their bodies. And each went straight forward. Wherever the spirit would go, they went, without turning as they went. . . .

And above the expanse over their heads there was the likeness of a throne, in appearance like sapphire; and seated above the likeness of a throne was a likeness with a human appearance. And upward from what had the appearance of his waist I saw as it were gleaming metal, like the appearance of fire enclosed all around. And downward from what had the appearance of his waist I saw as it were the appearance of fire, and there was brightness around him. Like the appearance of the bow that is in the cloud on the day of rain, so was the appearance of the brightness all around.

Such was the appearance of the likeness of the glory of the LORD. (1:4–28)

Israel is losing its land but not its Lord. In the midst of Ezekiel's despair, he sees God not as some pagan deity tied to the boundaries of Judah but as the awesome, omnipotent Lord of heaven and earth. The people have failed the Lord, but he will not fail them. Ezekiel, who wrote from about 593 to 571 BC,[1] straddled the eras before and after the fall of Jerusalem, reminding the people why it had occurred and calling them to repentance and ultimate hope.

Though the book is full of mysterious visions (a characteristic of other apocalyptic books, such as Daniel, Zechariah, and Revelation), the structure is straightforward. The first twenty-four chapters describe Ezekiel's calling (1–3) and his initial prophecies against unfaithful Judah (4–24), which has defiled the temple with idolatry (8) and is a wayward bride (16). The people must repent or die (18). Yet the nations, which the Lord has used to punish Israel, also stand under his judgment (25–32). The Lord then explains why the punishment of his people has come (33–35) and promises a future restoration (36–39).

The rest of Ezekiel describes an angel-guided vision of a

massive new temple in Jerusalem, unlike any that has ever stood in the City of David (40–48). Commentators are divided on whether this structure is meant to be taken literally or as a picture of God's promised presence with his people.[2] One thing is certain: as God's glory left the city that bears his name (11), so one day it will return (43).

Gospel signposts abound in Ezekiel. The people, who have failed, will receive a new heart and spirit (11:14–21; 36:26–27); a divine "shepherd" is promised (34:1–16); the valley of dry bones portends both national restoration and physical resurrection (37); and water flows from the new temple (47:1–12), anticipating the river of life flowing from the throne in Revelation 22. Ezekiel is called "Son of man" (2:1, 3; 3:1, 3–4), a favorite self-designation of Jesus.

As the key verse says, the Lord will bless his people not because of their righteousness—they have none—but because of his good pleasure and for his glory. It is a powerful reminder of God's grace, seen most clearly in Christ: "By grace you have been saved through faith. And this is not your own doing; it is the gift of God, not a result of works, so that no one may boast" (Eph. 2:8–9).

27

Daniel 6:26

I make a decree, that in all my royal dominion people
are to tremble and fear before the God of Daniel,

for he is the living God,
enduring forever;
his kingdom shall never be destroyed,
and his dominion shall be to the end.

DANIEL TELLS THE STORY OF GOD'S CONTINUING CARE FOR HIS people in a hostile world and his sovereignty over the nations and history. The author was among the first Jews taken captive to Babylon by Nebuchadnezzar in 605 BC, about a decade before the prophet Ezekiel was exiled and about two decades before the horrific destruction of Jerusalem during the time of Jeremiah. A faithful Jew, Daniel had a long career as an official in Babylon, serving until the Persian Empire took over in 539 BC.

The book's first six chapters illustrate how the Lord protected and exalted his faithful followers Daniel (renamed Belteshazzar), Hananiah (Shadrach), Mishael (Meshach), and Azariah (Abednego) in a pagan environment (1:1–7). Daniel and his friends resolve not to defile themselves with the royal food, and the Lord vindicates them: "In every matter of wisdom and understanding about which the king inquired of them, he found them ten times better than all the magicians and enchanters that were in all his kingdom" (1:20).

This evaluation is proved true in chapter 2, when Nebuchadnezzar has a secret dream about future world empires that only Daniel can interpret. Daniel wisely gives God the glory: "No wise men, enchanters, magicians, or astrologers can show to the king the mystery that the king has asked, but there is a God in heaven who reveals mysteries, and he has made known to King Nebuchadnezzar what will be in the latter days" (2:27–28).

Chapter 3 shows the God of heaven protecting Shadrach, Meshach, and Abednego from Nebuchadnezzar's idolatrous decree. As the king is threatening to throw them into a fiery furnace, the three exhibit faith that is a model for God's people who face persecution in any era. "If this be so," they say, "our God whom we serve is able to deliver us from the burning fiery furnace, and he will deliver us out of your hand, O king. But if not, be it known to you, O king, that we will not serve your gods or worship the golden image that you have set up" (3:17–18). Faithfulness, regardless of the circumstances, is not up for negotiation. God delivers his servants from death, and Nebuchadnezzar acknowledges God (3:24–4:3).

In chapter 4, a proud Nebuchadnezzar is humbled again. As predicted in a dream, the king was "driven from among men and ate grass like an ox, and his body was wet with the dew of heaven till his hair grew as long as eagles' feathers, and his nails were like birds' claws" (4:33). Eventually coming to his senses, a chastened Nebuchadnezzar praises God: "Now I, Nebuchadnezzar, praise and extol and honor the King of heaven, for all his works are right and his ways are just; and those who walk in pride he is able to humble" (4:37).

However, in chapter 5, one of Nebuchadnezzar's successors, Belshazzar, mocks God and sees the writing on the wall. Daniel interprets the script: "MENE, MENE, TEKEL, and PARSIN" (5:25): the kingdom has been found wanting, is ending, and is being "given up." That night Belshazzar loses the empire to the Medes and Persians—as well as his life.

Opponents entrap Daniel under the new regime, and Daniel is thrown to the lions (6:1–18). As happened with his three friends in the fiery furnace, Daniel is miraculously delivered (6:19–24). In the key verse, "King Darius," possibly a general of Cyrus the Great,[1] gives glory to "the living God," whose "dominion shall be to the end" (6:26). It is a recognition of divine reality already spoken by the great Nebuchadnezzar and a truth illustrated throughout Daniel. It also is a bulwark against doubt and despair for all God's people—past, present, and future.

The second half of the book, written as apocalyptic literature, presents a series of sometimes confusing visions (7–12). They further illustrate that God remains sovereign over the empires of the earth and will deliver and use his people for his glory as history moves toward its sometimes perplexing but still predetermined end, the ultimate triumph of the kingdom of God. Daniel says, "I heard, but I did not understand. Then I said, 'O my lord, what shall be the outcome of these things?' [The angel] said, 'Go your way, Daniel, for the words are shut up and sealed until the time of the end. . . . But go your way till the end. And you shall rest and shall stand in your allotted place at the end of the days'" (12:8–9, 13).

While, like Daniel, God's people may sometimes be perplexed in the midst of their Lord's inscrutable doings, ultimately we can rest in the knowledge that all remains under his control.

28

Hosea 6:4

What shall I do with you, O Ephraim?
What shall I do with you, O Judah?
Your love is like a morning cloud,
like the dew that goes early away.

HOSEA IS THE FIRST OF WHAT ARE CALLED THE MINOR PROPHETS because of the generally shorter length of these twelve books at the end of the Old Testament compared with Isaiah, Jeremiah, Ezekiel, and Daniel. Hosea, unlike most other prophetic books, is focused on the Northern Kingdom, also known as Israel or Ephraim. Hosea reveals God's anger and compassion for his wayward people.

Hosea writes when Israel is crumbling. The nation, formed when the kingdom split after the reign of Solomon in 931 BC, has never been faithful to the Lord, though it has experienced spectacular grace from prophets such as Elijah, Elisha, and Hosea. Jeroboam II, a strong leader, has left the scene, succeeded by six monarchs in about thirty years. The cruel Assyrian Empire is rising just to the north, but Israel is too caught up in its own sin to see the divine judgment looming. So the Lord sends Hosea.

At the start of his ministry, Hosea is told to take Gomer, a prostitute, as his wife, "for the land commits great whoredom by forsaking the LORD" (1:2). Hosea will experience the unfaithfulness of the people to their God. The first child is named Jezreel.

Then the relationship between God and his people fails. The next child is born to Gomer (but not Hosea) and is called No Mercy: God's judgment is coming. Another is called Not My People: God and Israel will soon be parted (1:4–9).

Hosea's painful personal story continues for three chapters, followed by eleven chapters warning of judgment. Yet the book is not completely dark. Though God must punish, he expresses an urgent desire for mercy throughout:

> Yet the number of the children of Israel shall be like the sand of the sea, which cannot be measured or numbered. And in the place where it was said to them, "You are not my people," it shall be said to them, "Children of the living God." And the children of Judah and the children of Israel shall be gathered together, and they shall appoint for themselves one head. And they shall go up from the land, for great shall be the day of Jezreel. (1:10–11)

God pursues his people with incredible passion.

> *What shall I do with you, O Ephraim?*
> *What shall I do with you, O Judah?*
> *Your love is like a morning cloud,*
> *like the dew that goes early away.*
> *Therefore I have hewn them by the prophets;*
> *I have slain them by the words of my mouth,*
> *and my judgment goes forth as the light.*
> *For I desire steadfast love and not sacrifice,*
> *the knowledge of God rather than burnt offerings.*
>
> *But like Adam they transgressed the covenant;*
> *there they dealt faithlessly with me. (6:4–7)*

God is not some soulless deity, an eye in the sky keeping track of all our movements in order to deal out punishment. He is a betrayed Husband, a jilted Lover, who nevertheless desires mercy for us, even to the end.

Yet the end finally comes. Assyria destroys the Northern Kingdom and carries off its people in 722 BC. Israel disappears from the pages of history but not from the heart of God:

> How can I give you up, O Ephraim?
>> How can I hand you over, O Israel?
> How can I make you like Admah?
>> How can I treat you like Zeboiim?
> My heart recoils within me;
>> my compassion grows warm and tender.
> I will not execute my burning anger;
>> I will not again destroy Ephraim;
> for I am God and not a man,
>> the Holy One in your midst,
>> and I will not come in wrath.
>
> They shall go after the LORD;
>> he will roar like a lion;
> when he roars,
>> his children shall come trembling from the west;
> they shall come trembling like birds from Egypt,
>> and like doves from the land of Assyria,
>> and I will return them to their homes, declares the LORD.
> (11:8–11)

Somehow, the Lord will bring his wayward people back, even those seemingly dispersed among the nations. God's mercy will triumph over his judgment (James 2:13):

> *I will heal their apostasy;*
> *I will love them freely,*
> *for my anger has turned from them....*
> *[T]hey shall flourish like the grain;*
> *they shall blossom like the vine;*
> *their fame shall be like the wine of Lebanon.*
>   *(Hos. 14:4–7)*

God's prevailing mercy in Hosea foreshadows an even greater spiritual restoration when the Jewish people turn to their Messiah: "A partial hardening has come upon Israel, until the fullness of the Gentiles has come in. And in this way all Israel will be saved" (Rom. 11:25–26).

29

Joel 2:28

It shall come to pass afterward,
that I will pour out my Spirit on all flesh;
your sons and your daughters shall prophesy,
your old men shall dream dreams,
and your young men shall see visions.

NO ONE KNOWS WITH CERTAINTY WHEN JOEL WROTE HIS STARTLING prophecy of doom and grace, though many regard this short book as the earliest of the prophetic books. But most commentators agree that it begins with a vivid and terrifying description of a devastating locust invasion in Judah:

What the cutting locust left,
the swarming locust has eaten.
What the swarming locust left,
the hopping locust has eaten,
and what the hopping locust left,
the destroying locust has eaten. (1:4)

This is no mere agricultural tragedy, a blind outcome of the laws of nature. The invasion is nothing less than the judgment of God:

> Put on sackcloth and lament, O priests;
> wail, O ministers of the altar. . . .

> Alas for the day!
> For the day of the LORD is near,
> and as destruction from the Almighty it comes.
> (1:13, 15)

The "day of the LORD" figures prominently in Joel. The concept can refer to a locust infestation (1:15) or a larger judgment of God against his people (2:1–11) or the nations (3:14). "However, for God's people, it is also associated with his presence (2:27), blessing (3:18), and salvation (2:31–32; 3:16)."[1] So the character of "the day" depends upon the character of the people to whom it comes.

Chapter 2 moves beyond the locust invasion to an even greater national calamity—the unstoppable invasion of an implacable army:

> Let all the inhabitants of the land tremble,
> for the day of the LORD is coming; it is near,
> a day of darkness and gloom,
> a day of clouds and thick darkness!
> Like blackness there is spread upon the mountains
> a great and powerful people;
> their like has never been before,
> nor will be again after them
> through the years of all generations. (2:1–2)

We don't know whether this attack occurred with the Babylonians in 586 BC, the sacking of Jerusalem in AD 70, or will happen in the future. We do know, however, that the Lord seeks the repentance and restoration of his people:

> *"Yet even now," declares the* LORD,
>> *"return to me with all your heart,*
> *with fasting, with weeping, and with mourning;*
>> *and rend your hearts and not your garments." (2:12–13)*

Joel looks ahead to a day when the Lord will rescue and provide for his people—not just externally, against invading armies, but internally, against the prevailing power of sin:

> *It shall come to pass afterward,*
>> *that I will pour out my Spirit on all flesh;*
> *your sons and your daughters shall prophesy,*
>> *your old men shall dream dreams,*
>> *and your young men shall see visions.*
> *Even on the male and female servants*
>> *in those days I will pour out my Spirit.*

And I will show wonders in the heavens and on the earth, blood and fire and columns of smoke. The sun shall be turned to darkness, and the moon to blood, before the great and awesome day of the LORD comes. And it shall come to pass that everyone who calls on the name of the LORD shall be saved. (2:28–32)

It is a promise seen in Isaiah (32:15; 44:3) and Ezekiel (39:29)[2] and fulfilled on another "day"—the day of pentecost, when the Spirit is given to the church (Acts 2:17–21). Peter stands up in Jerusalem, only a few short weeks after the crucifixion and the resurrection, and explains this new day in God's dealings with mankind, saying that it is the fulfillment of Joel's ancient prophecy. His audience, Jews from around the world, agrees—and some three thousand souls call upon the Lord and are saved (Acts 2:41).

The only promise the wicked receive from Joel, however, is that the day of the Lord will be a time for judgment, even as everyone who calls on him *will* be saved:

> Multitudes, multitudes,
> in the valley of decision!
> For the day of the LORD is near
> in the valley of decision.
> The sun and the moon are darkened,
> and the stars withdraw their shining.
>
> The LORD roars from Zion,
> and utters his voice from Jerusalem,
> and the heavens and the earth quake.
> But the LORD is a refuge to his people,
> a stronghold to the people of Israel. (3:14–16)

The promised outpouring of the Holy Spirit in the hearts of believers, promised in our key verse, is the Lord's pledge that he will be an eternal refuge for his people (2 Cor. 1:21–22).

30

Amos 5:24

Let justice roll down like waters,
and righteousness like an ever-flowing stream.

WITH ASSYRIA'S REGIONAL DOMINANCE IN CHECK FOR THE TIME being, Israel is experiencing a renaissance of material prosperity under Jeroboam II. However, the Lord sends the Northern Kingdom the prophet Amos, a shepherd from the southern backwater of Tekoa (1:1), to warn the people of coming judgment (1:2).

His prophecy seemingly starts out well. That's because the Lord's initial targets are Israel's pagan neighbors: Damascus (1:3–5), Gaza (1:6–8), Tyre (1:9–10), Edom (1:11–12), Rabbah (1:13–15), and Moab (2:1–3).

God holds these nations accountable for their sins, even though they do not have the Law. As Paul would say later, "The wrath of God is revealed from heaven against all ungodliness and unrighteousness of men, who by their unrighteousness suppress the truth" (Rom. 1:18).

Amos's announcement of doom begins with the same formula for each: "For three transgressions . . . , and for four, I will not revoke the punishment" (Amos 1:3). The Lord is keeping a careful accounting of their sins. And these nations are indeed guilty before God, committing such outrages as carrying whole peoples into exile and ripping open the bellies of pregnant women.

Then the Lord's judgment moves uncomfortably closer: "For three transgressions of Judah, and for four, I will not revoke the punishment" (2:4–5). Judah, where Solomon's temple stands, faces a devouring fire for rejecting God's law. Even the pagans have not done this! If the Southern Kingdom stands condemned, what hope does Samaria have? And indeed, the sentence is swiftly pronounced:

> For three transgressions of Israel,
>> and for four, I will not revoke the punishment,
> because they sell the righteous for silver,
>> and the needy for a pair of sandals—
> those who trample the head of the poor into the dust of
> the earth
>> and turn aside the way of the afflicted;
> a man and his father go in to the same girl,
>> so that my holy name is profaned. (2:6–7)

Israel's original sin, if you will, was Jeroboam I's rejection of the true God for the syncretistic pagan worship of golden calves (1 Kings 12:25–33). But the Lord's indictment begins with some of the fruit of this suppression of the truth—greed, social oppression, and sexual sin. Wealthy Israel is spiritually bankrupt. As Jesus says to the church at Laodicea, "You say, I am rich, I have prospered, and I need nothing, not realizing that you are wretched, pitiable, poor, blind, and naked" (Rev. 3:17).

The result will be national ruin:

> An adversary shall surround the land
>> and bring down your defenses from you,
> and your strongholds shall be plundered. (Amos 3:11)

Further, he tells the wealthy women, whom he calls "cows of Bashan," seemingly at ease in the lap of luxury:

> The Lord GOD has sworn by his holiness
> that, behold, the days are coming upon you,
> when they shall take you away with hooks,
> even the last of you with fishhooks. (4:2)

These "cows" are about to be slaughtered. The people believe, because of their special history, that they have a license to sin—against both God and their fellow man. They are looking forward to a "day of the LORD" when they will be delivered from all their foes. But the Lord says that they bear special responsibility (3:2). Therefore, the "day of the LORD" for them will be one of judgment:

> Woe to you who desire the day of the LORD!
> Why would you have the day of the LORD?
> It is darkness, and not light. (5:18)

How are the people to avoid this disaster? First, they must abandon mere outward worship (5:21–23). Second, the key verse says that they must forsake their oppressive ways: "Let justice roll down like waters, / and righteousness like an ever-flowing stream" (5:24).

The people must show their change of heart toward God by the way they treat their fellow Israelites. John asked, "If anyone says, 'I love God,' and hates his brother, he is a liar; for he who does not love his brother whom he has seen cannot love God whom he has not seen" (1 John 4:20). A concern for justice is a critical indicator of spiritual life.

Will the people repent, changing both heart and action? Amos is skeptical for the short term (9:8–11) but ultimately hopeful.

Assyria indeed came in 722 BC and carried out God's judgment against Israel, uprooting and scattering the nation to the four winds. Yet, somehow, God's forgiven and redeemed people will return: "I will restore the fortunes of my people Israel. . . . I will plant them on their land" (9:14–15).

31

Obadiah 4

Though you soar aloft like the eagle,
*   though your nest is set among the stars,*
*   from there I will bring you down,*
declares the LORD.

OBADIAH IS THE SHORTEST BOOK IN THE OLD TESTAMENT, BUT ITS message is definitely not the sweetest. The author is pronouncing judgment on the small mountain-kingdom of Edom, founded by Jacob's brother, Esau, and directly to the southeast of Jerusalem and the Dead Sea. The crime is treachery.

When Jerusalem fell to Babylon in 586 BC, the Edomites not only stepped aside and did nothing, they joined in the looting and "handed over captives to Babylon, and possessed lands in the Negeb area to the south."[1] It was the final chapter in the perpetual battle between Esau and Jacob:

> *Because of the violence done to your brother Jacob,*
> *   shame shall cover you,*
> *   and you shall be cut off forever.*
> *On the day that you stood aloof,*
> *   on the day that strangers carried off his wealth*
> *and foreigners entered his gates*
> *   and cast lots for Jerusalem,*
> *   you were like one of them. (10–11)*

Because Edomite cities were cunningly accessible only via winding, narrow paths, the inhabitants felt secure in their mountain strongholds, which were up to five thousand feet above sea level[2]—difficult for an army to reach. Edom's fortresses were "practically impregnable from the assault of enemies."[3] The people thought they were secure. Obadiah accurately reports the smugness of Edom and the Lord's holy response:

> *The pride of your heart has deceived you,*
> > *you who live in the clefts of the rock,*
> > *in your lofty dwelling,*
> *who say in your heart,*
> > *"Who will bring me down to the ground?"*
> *Though you soar aloft like the eagle,*
> > *though your nest is set among the stars,*
> > *from there I will bring you down. (3–4)*

Notwithstanding its natural defenses, Edom's doom is sure, Obadiah says:

> *The day of the LORD is near upon all the nations.*
> *As you have done, it shall be done to you;*
> > *your deeds shall return on your own head. (15)*

Edom betrayed Judah and would itself be betrayed, leading to its utter destruction:

> *If thieves came to you,*
> > *if plunderers came by night—*
> > *how you have been destroyed!—*
> > *would they not steal only enough for themselves?*
> *If grape gatherers came to you,*
> > *would they not leave gleanings?*

How Esau has been pillaged,
his treasures sought out!
All your allies have driven you to your border;
those at peace with you have deceived you;
they have prevailed against you;
those who eat your bread have set a trap beneath you—
you have no understanding.

Will I not on that day, declares the LORD,
destroy the wise men out of Edom,
and understanding out of Mount Esau?
And your mighty men shall be dismayed, O Teman,
so that every man from Mount Esau will be cut off by
slaughter. (5–9)

For a while, at least, Edom's pride goes unpunished. While Ammon and Moab quickly fall to Babylon, Edom remains unmolested in its mountain aerie. But in 553 BC, Nabonidus, the final king of Babylon, finds a way in, "leaving a carving on a remote cliff not far from the capital Bozrah . . . to mark his triumph. Signs of destruction by fire from that time have been found in some Edomite towns, and . . . the kingdom of Edom ended."[4]

Yet Obadiah has a word of hope for the people of God who have been carried off to Babylon. They will one day annex the land of the God haters and serve the Lord and his triumphant kingdom:

Those of the Negeb shall possess Mount Esau,
and those of the Shephelah shall possess the land of the
Philistines;
they shall possess the land of Ephraim and the land
of Samaria,
and Benjamin shall possess Gilead.

The exiles of this host of the people of Israel
*   shall possess the land of the Canaanites as far*
*   as Zarephath,*
and the exiles of Jerusalem who are in Sepharad
*   shall possess the cities of the Negeb.*
Saviors shall go up to Mount Zion
*   to rule Mount Esau,*
*   and the kingdom shall be the* LORD's. *(19–21)*

The divergent fates of Edom and Israel illustrate a perennial biblical principle: "He gives more grace. Therefore it says, 'God opposes the proud, but gives grace to the humble.' . . . Humble yourselves before the Lord, and he will exalt you" (James 4:6, 10).

32

Jonah 4:2

He prayed to the LORD and said, "O LORD, is not this
what I said when I was yet in my country? That is why
I made haste to flee to Tarshish; for I knew that you
are a gracious God and merciful, slow to anger and
abounding in steadfast love, and relenting from disaster."

THE LORD SENDS JONAH WITH A MESSAGE TO NINEVEH, AN ANCIENT
city about five hundred miles northeast of Israel, in the heart of
the wicked Assyrian Empire: "Arise, go to Nineveh, that great
city, and call out against it, for their evil has come up before
me" (1:2).

Instead, for reasons not immediately known, Jonah boards a
ship and flees in the opposite direction, "away from the presence
of the LORD" (1:3). But God whips up a storm, and Jonah's sailing
companions are forced to throw him overboard to save their own
lives (1:4–15). The sea calms immediately.

Ironically, though Jonah the Israelite prophet is resisting
God's call, the pagan sailors "feared the LORD exceedingly, and
they offered a sacrifice to the LORD and made vows" (1:16). In
mercy, God sends Jonah "a great fish" (1:17) to bring the disobedient but now grateful prophet (2) back to his task:

"Then the word of the LORD came to Jonah the second time,
saying, 'Arise, go to Nineveh, that great city, and call out against it

the message that I tell you.' So Jonah arose and went to Nineveh, according to the word of the Lord. . . . And he called out, 'Yet forty days, and Nineveh shall be overthrown!'" (3:1–4).

The shocking response of the Assyrians is instantaneous—not scorn or persecution but repentance. They are hoping against hope that God might change his mind. "Who knows?" the king says helplessly. "God may turn and relent and turn from his fierce anger, so that we may not perish" (3:9). And indeed the Lord *does* relent (3:10).

However, Jonah now prays, *"O Lord, is not this what I said when I was yet in my country? That is why I made haste to flee to Tarshish; for I knew that you are a gracious God and merciful, slow to anger and abounding in steadfast love, and relenting from disaster. Therefore now, O Lord, please take my life from me, for it is better for me to die than to live"* (4:2–3, emphasis added).

Now we know why Jonah ran. He fears not the wrath of the Assyrians but the mercy of the Lord, repeating to God the name given to Moses: "The Lord, the Lord, a God merciful and gracious, slow to anger, and abounding in steadfast love and faithfulness, keeping steadfast love for thousands, forgiving iniquity and transgression and sin, but who will by no means clear the guilty, visiting the iniquity of the fathers on the children and the children's children, to the third and the fourth generation" (Ex. 34:6–7).

God is not a mere tribal deity, rewarding his followers and terrifying his enemies. No, he loves *all* his creatures. As Jesus tells the woman of Samaria (another supposed outsider to the divine blessings), "God is spirit, and those who worship him must worship in spirit and truth" (John 4:24).

Many of the prophets of Israel would have given their right arms to see such a spiritual response to their preaching. Jonah, however, wants nothing more than for the Assyrians to ignore his warning—and go to hell. In this, he is definitely *not* godlike.

The Lord graciously seeks to change the heart of his hateful, unforgiving prophet (Jonah 4:4), providing a demonstration of Jonah's misplaced priorities (4:5–9). The Lord sends a plant that gives Jonah much-needed shade outside the city. Then God sends a worm, which kills the plant. Jonah, overwrought, again asks to die. God attempts to shame Jonah into compassion: "You pity the plant, for which you did not labor, nor did you make it grow, which came into being in a night and perished in a night. And should not I pity Nineveh, that great city, in which there are more than 120,000 persons who do not know their right hand from their left, and also much cattle?" (4:10–11).

God had blessed his people to be a blessing to the nations. Will Israel obey?

33

Micah 6:8

He has told you, O man, what is good;
and what does the Lord require of you
but to do justice, and to love kindness,
and to walk humbly with your God?

MICAH PROPHESIED IN LARGELY THE SAME ERA AS ISAIAH AND Amos. Accordingly, he was present for the Northern Kingdom's long-awaited disaster at the hands of Assyria as well as the Southern Kingdom's deliverance from the same group. Yet Micah does not give tiny Judah a pass. Its sins are grave, and judgment still looms unless the people forsake their false religion and follow the Lord from their hearts.

In the first of three indictments (1–2; 3–5; 6–7), Micah calls on Samaria (Israel) and Judah to repent:

Woe to those who devise wickedness
and work evil on their beds!
When the morning dawns, they perform it,
because it is in the power of their hand.
They covet fields and seize them,
and houses, and take them away;
they oppress a man and his house,
a man and his inheritance. (2:1–2)

It is a message of social justice, like that of Amos, which the guilty do not wish to hear:

> *"Do not preach"—thus they preach—*
> *   "one should not preach of such things;*
> *   disgrace will not overtake us."*
> *Should this be said, O house of Jacob? . . .*
> *Do not my words do good*
> *   to him who walks uprightly?*
> *But lately my people have risen up as an enemy;*
> *you strip the rich robe from those who pass by trustingly*
> *   with no thought of war. (2:6–8)*

In the next indictment, Micah calls out the leaders and prophets with even more irony. It turns out that the oppressing people are getting the rulers they deserve:

> *Is it not for you to know justice?—*
> *   you who hate the good and love the evil,*
> *   who tear the skin from off my people*
> *   and their flesh from off their bones,*
> *   who eat the flesh of my people,*
> *   and flay their skin from off them,*
> *   and break their bones in pieces*
> *   and chop them up like meat in a pot,*
> *   like flesh in a cauldron. (3:1–3)*

Those who have rejected the Lord, as shown by their oppression of their brothers, will in turn be rejected by him (3:4). The false prophets, those who "declare war against [God]" (3:5), face the same terrifying fate—the absence of the Lord from their lives and ministries:

> *It shall be night to you, without vision,*
> *and darkness to you, without divination.*
> *The sun shall go down on the prophets,*
> *and the day shall be black over them;*
> *the seers shall be disgraced,*
> *and the diviners put to shame;*
> *they shall all cover their lips,*
> *for there is no answer from God. (3:6–7)*

The contrast with the ministry of Micah is both striking and condemning:

> *But as for me, I am filled with power,*
> *with the Spirit of the* LORD,
> *and with justice and might,*
> *to declare to Jacob his transgression*
> *and to Israel his sin. (3:8)*

Micah shows the guilty that true religion is a matter of both moral power (justice) and spiritual power (might). You cannot have one without the other. That is why the people's religion, although outwardly sacrificial, is so thoroughly powerless. He paraphrases their questions about why the Lord has departed from among them (6:6–7) and then, in the key verse, provides the inescapable answer.

> *He has told you, O man, what is good;*
> *and what does the* LORD *require of you*
> *but to do justice, and to love kindness,*
> *and to walk humbly with your God? (6:8)*

In the New Testament, James would say the same: "Religion that is pure and undefiled before God, the Father, is this: to visit orphans and widows in their affliction, and to keep oneself unstained from the world" (1:27).

But because the people have rebelled, the Lord will bring disaster: "Zion shall be plowed as a field; / Jerusalem shall become a heap of ruins" (Mic. 3:12, quoted as prophecy by Jeremiah [26:18] nearly two centuries later). Yet one day the Lord will provide a "shepherd," born in Bethlehem, who will finally bring peace and righteousness to his people (5:2–5).

34

Nahum 1:3

The LORD is slow to anger and great in power,
and the LORD will by no means clear the guilty.
His way is in whirlwind and storm,
and the clouds are the dust of his feet.

IF JONAH REPRESENTS A TEMPORARY REPRIEVE FOR NINEVEH, NAHUM predicts the city's ultimate destruction a century and a half later. The opening words of Nahum's prophecy are an about-face from the Lord's earlier decision of mercy:

The LORD is a jealous and avenging God;
the LORD is avenging and wrathful;
the LORD takes vengeance on his adversaries
and keeps wrath for his enemies.
The LORD is slow to anger and great in power,
and the LORD will by no means clear the guilty.
His way is in whirlwind and storm,
and the clouds are the dust of his feet. (1:2–3)

The words hit Assyria like slaps to the face: "jealous," "avenging," and "wrathful." Time is up for Nineveh, Assyria's "great city" (Jonah 1:2), once graciously spared by God. Though "the LORD is slow to anger," he "will by no means clear the guilty."

This statement of God's character is a dark echo of Jonah's earlier words of accusation against God's kindness: "I knew that you are a gracious God and merciful, slow to anger and abounding in steadfast love, and relenting from disaster" (Jonah 4:2). It recalls the warning in God's name given to Moses "The LORD . . . who will by no means clear the guilty, visiting the iniquity of the fathers on the children and the children's children, to the third and the fourth generation" (Ex. 34:6–7).

The list of Nineveh's sins is damning: vile idolatry (Nah. 1:14; 3:4); violence, lying, and greed (3:1); and constant evil (3:19). The pagan Assyrian Empire, the world's first military dictatorship, which destroyed the Northern Kingdom in 722 BC and attempted to wipe out Judah as well, had made itself an adversary of God, and God noticed:

> *With an overflowing flood*
> *he will make a complete end of the adversaries,*
> *and will pursue his enemies into darkness. (1:8)*

The Lord, in fact, is about to cleanse the world of the brutal Assyrians "with an overflowing flood":

> *The river gates are opened;*
> *the palace melts away;*
> *its mistress is stripped; she is carried off,*
> *her slave girls lamenting,*
> *moaning like doves*
> *and beating their breasts.*
> *Nineveh is like a pool*
> *whose waters run away.*
> *"Halt! Halt!" they cry,*
> *but none turns back.*

Plunder the silver,
plunder the gold!
There is no end of the treasure
or of the wealth of all precious things.

Desolate! Desolation and ruin!
Hearts melt and knees tremble;
anguish is in all loins;
all faces grow pale! (2:6–10)

The predicted desolation of the jewel of Assyria will be complete: "she became an exile"; "her infants were dashed in pieces"; "your troops are women in your midst"; and "fire has devoured your bars" (3:10–13). Nineveh's destruction happened, just as predicted by Nahum:

> Historians . . . tell us about the remarkable fall of the mighty metropolis in 612 BC. The Babylonians and the Medes, two rising powers, marched on Nineveh. Conventional means of attack were futile, so their armies dammed the rivers that flowed into the city. The pent-up water was suddenly released, smashing through one of the outer walls. The invaders then looted Nineveh, leaving only "heaps of debris."[1]

God's blessing removed, the curse pronounced in 3:1 ("Woe to the bloody city . . . !") finally arrived. Justice means giving people their due, whether good or bad. And while the Lord's justice may sometimes be delayed in our fallen world, it is never denied, even for mighty Nineveh. Such judgments in history prefigure an ultimate Judgment Day.

At the end of the book, the prophet depicts a righteous celebration over Nineveh's fall:

There is no easing your hurt;
your wound is grievous.
All who hear the news about you
clap their hands over you.
For upon whom has not come
your unceasing evil? (3:19)

It is a precursor to the martyred saints' cry for justice in heaven: "O Sovereign Lord, holy and true," they cry out, "how long before you will judge and avenge our blood on those who dwell on the earth?" (Rev. 6:10). Without a firm grasp of the justice of God, we will never understand the need for his grace.

35

Habakkuk 3:16

I hear, and my body trembles;
my lips quiver at the sound;
rottenness enters into my bones;
my legs tremble beneath me.
Yet I will quietly wait for the day of trouble
to come upon people who invade us.

HABAKKUK PROVES THE OLD ADAGE "BE CAREFUL WHAT YOU WISH for because you just might get it." Writing in the final years of Judah's spiritual decline but before the Babylonian invasion, the prophet rails about the rampant unrighteousness among God's people:

O LORD, how long shall I cry for help,
and you will not hear?
Or cry to you "Violence!"
and you will not save?
Why do you make me see iniquity,
and why do you idly look at wrong? (1:2–3)

The land is filled with oppression, violence, iniquity, destruction, strife, contention, a "paralyzed" law, and "perverted" justice. The problem, the prophet says, is that "justice never goes forth."

Yet the Lord "idly look[s] at wrong" (1:3–4). It is a stinging indict-ment of a supposedly distant, indifferent God.

In his response, the Lord sets Habakkuk straight. He does care about Israel's sin, but he is about to do something unexpected:

> Look among the nations, and see;
>> wonder and be astounded.
> For I am doing a work in your days
>> that you would not believe if told.
> For behold, I am raising up the Chaldeans,
>> that bitter and hasty nation,
> who march through the breadth of the earth,
>> to seize dwellings not their own. (1:5–6)

Habakkuk is well acquainted with the Chaldeans (another name for the Babylonians). They are the new geopolitical power on the block. The prophet knows, however, that God is "raising up" Babylon not just to punish Assyria for its sin (see Nahum) but to judge tiny Judah for its transgressions. Though the Lord has not specifically spelled out this plan, the prophet knows what is coming:

> Are you not from everlasting,
>> O LORD my God, my Holy One?
>> We shall not die.
> O LORD, you have ordained them as a judgment,
>> and you, O Rock, have established them for reproof.
>> (1:12)

Still, Habakkuk, in this second complaint, again accuses the Lord of idle indifference in the face of evil, rightly pointing out that the Chaldeans are bigger sinners than the Israelites:

You who are of purer eyes than to see evil
and cannot look at wrong,
why do you idly look at traitors
and remain silent when the wicked swallows up
the man more righteous than he? (1:13)

It's not fair, Habakkuk is saying. The Babylonians are like a rapacious fisherman, capturing the nations in his net (to which he gives thanks), and then mercilessly living in luxury at their expense "forever" (1:14–17). Hoping to convince a just God to change his plan, the prophet now awaits the divine reply:

I will take my stand at my watchpost
and station myself on the tower,
and look out to see what he will say to me,
and what I will answer concerning my complaint. (2:1)

The Lord's answer is not what Habakkuk expects—or desires. God is going to fairly judge the world and Babylon in his own time (2:2–20), and he tells the prophet, "If it seems slow, wait for it" (2:3). Then God contrasts the patient, trusting response he expects of his people in the midst of their perplexity with the arrogance of Babylon: "Behold, his soul is puffed up; it is not upright within him, / but the righteous shall live by his faith" (2:4).

It is a call to trust God that sees its full expression in a person's faithful response to the gospel of Christ (Rom. 1:17; Gal. 3:11). We are to believe the Lord's diagnosis of our sinful condition and cling to him, no matter what. This Habakkuk does, the key verse says, despite the coming judgment of his sinful people by an even more unrighteous Babylon. It is the proverbial bitter pill for the prophet:

> *I hear, and my body trembles;*
> *   my lips quiver at the sound;*
> *rottenness enters into my bones;*
> *   my legs tremble beneath me.*
> *Yet I will quietly wait for the day of trouble*
> *   to come upon people who invade us. (3:16)*

Habakkuk's faith in the Lord emerges stronger than ever. Gone are his accusations and slurs, replaced by a soaring, world-conquering trust, despite the circumstances:

> *Though the fig tree should not blossom,*
> *   nor fruit be on the vines,*
> *the produce of the olive fail*
> *   and the fields yield no food,*
> *the flock be cut off from the fold*
> *   and there be no herd in the stalls,*
> *yet I will rejoice in the LORD;*
> *   I will take joy in the God of my salvation.*
> *GOD, the Lord, is my strength;*
> *   he makes my feet like the deer's;*
> *   he makes me tread on my high places. (3:17–19)*

Habakkuk gives us permission to take our hard questions and our doubts to the Lord. Though we don't always get what we ask for, in the end we can rest in God's wisdom and plan.

36

Zephaniah 3:7

> I said, "Surely you will fear me;
>   you will accept correction.
> Then your dwelling would not be cut off
>   according to all that I have appointed against you."
> But all the more they were eager
>   to make all their deeds corrupt.

KING JOSIAH, A GODLY RULER, HAS ASSUMED THE THRONE AND IS attempting a last-ditch reformation. He is repairing the dilapidated temple, returning God's Word to the people, putting an end to lingering paganism in the land, and reinstituting the Passover (2 Kings 22–23). But the Southern Kingdom's future is very much in doubt. Is it too late to repent?

Speaking for the Lord with a series of chilling "I wills," Zephaniah makes clear that Judah and the nations are in the same boat—guilty—and will face utter devastation:

> "I will utterly sweep away everything
>   from the face of the earth," declares the LORD.
> "I will sweep away man and beast;
>   I will sweep away the birds of the heavens
>   and the fish of the sea,
> and the rubble with the wicked.

> *I will cut off mankind*
> *from the face of the earth," declares the* LORD.
> *"I will stretch out my hand against Judah*
> *and against all the inhabitants of Jerusalem." (1:2–4)*

The Philistine cities of Gaza, Ashkelon, Ashdod, and Ekron "shall be deserted . . . a desolation . . . driven out . . . uprooted . . . until no inhabitant is left" (2:4–5). Moab and Ammon will become "like Sodom . . . [and] Gomorrah, a land possessed by nettles and salt pits" for their proud boasting (2:8–10). Cush and Assyria, still dominant, will also experience disaster (2:12–13).

Judah, too, faces its comeuppance—for its idolatry, its injustice, and its complacency. The day of the Lord is coming for the chosen people (1:7, 12–14).

The Lord describes Jerusalem, the very focus of his presence on earth, in the harshest terms (3:1–2), but according to our key verse, God's intention was always to bless his people, although they refused:

> *I said, "Surely you will fear me;*
> *you will accept correction.*
> *Then your dwelling would not be cut off*
> *according to all that I have appointed against you."*
> *But all the more they were eager*
> *to make all their deeds corrupt. (3:7)*

Or as the Lord Jesus would later say ahead of a future judgment against the city, "O Jerusalem, Jerusalem, the city that kills the prophets and stones those who are sent to it! How often would I have gathered your children together as a hen gathers her brood under her wings, and you were not willing!" (Luke 13:34).

The day of the Lord is coming, though God recognizes that

even at this late date some in the land remain faithful. National repentance is out of the question, and yet a remnant may escape:

> *Seek the LORD, all you humble of the land,*
>> *who do his just commands;*
> *seek righteousness; seek humility;*
>> *perhaps you may be hidden*
>> *on the day of the anger of the LORD. (2:3)*

Though unnamed by Zephaniah, eventually Babylon came, destroying Jerusalem and most of the surrounding nations within a few decades (3:8).

But the King's intention to bless will not be denied for Israel and the nations:

> *"At that time I will change the speech of the peoples*
>> *to a pure speech,*
> *that all of them may call upon the name of the LORD*
>> *and serve him with one accord." . . .*

> *The King of Israel, the LORD, is in your midst;*
>> *you shall never again fear evil. . . .*
> *The LORD your God is in your midst,*
>> *a mighty one who will save;*
> *he will rejoice over you with gladness;*
>> *he will quiet you by his love;*
> *he will exult over you with loud singing. (3:9, 15, 17)*

This prophecy of divine presence and joy will find its ultimate fulfillment in the future, when God will "wipe away every tear" from our eyes (Rev. 21:4).

37

Haggai 1:4

Is it a time for you yourselves to dwell in your
paneled houses, while this house lies in ruins?

ISRAEL OUGHT TO HAVE LEARNED ITS LESSON. A PEOPLE RESCUED
from Egyptian slavery and graciously given God's Law and a land
in which to practice it should have fulfilled its calling to lead the
nations to God, "for the earth shall be full of the knowledge of the
LORD as the waters cover the sea" (Isa. 11:9).

Instead, the kingdom established by David split into two
kingdoms (931 BC) and was destroyed by those very nations, first
by Assyria in the north (722 BC) and then, even more astonish-
ingly, by Babylon in the south (586 BC). Jerusalem and Solomon's
temple were laid waste by Nebuchadnezzar, and the remnant of
God's people was forced into exile.

This disaster happened because the people had forgotten the
Lord and brought upon themselves the fearsome curses predicted
by Moses:

> If you will not obey the voice of the LORD your God or be
> careful to do all his commandments and his statutes that I
> command you today, then all these curses shall come upon you
> and overtake you. Cursed shall you be in the city, and cursed
> shall you be in the field. . . . The LORD will bring you and your

king whom you set over you to a nation that neither you nor your fathers have known. And there you shall serve other gods of wood and stone. And you shall become a horror, a proverb, and a byword among all the peoples where the LORD will lead you away. (Deut. 28:15–16, 36–37)

Yet God's severe chastening came to an end when Cyrus, king of Persia, proclaimed in 538 BC that the Jews could return to their land and rebuild the temple. And some, led by godly men such as Zerubbabel, did return. But life as a subject people was hard, and the temple reconstruction languished. The people were struggling to rub two shekels together and began to focus more on their own needs than on God's glory.

Haggai enters at this point—520 BC. Speaking to Zerubbabel, the governor, and Joshua, son of the high priest, Haggai diagnoses the problem. They have failed to rebuild God's house. "Consider your ways," Haggai tells them (1:5, 7). He also asks,

Is it a time for you yourselves to dwell in your paneled houses, while this house lies in ruins? . . . You have sown much, and harvested little. You eat, but you never have enough; you drink, but you never have your fill. You clothe yourselves, but no one is warm. And he who earns wages does so to put them into a bag with holes. (1:4, 6, emphasis added)

The people are in misery not because the local economy is bad (though it is) but because they have been unfaithful to God and his covenant—precisely what drove them into exile in the first place. "Therefore," God says, "the heavens above you have withheld the dew, and the earth has withheld its produce" (1:10).

This theme comes to full fruition in the New Testament. Acknowledging that our desire to provide for ourselves is legitimate, Jesus nonetheless said that God honors those who give *him* first place: "Seek first the kingdom of God and his righteousness, and all these things will be added to you" (Matt. 6:33).

The leaders and people take Haggai's message to heart and begin to rebuild (Hag. 1:12–15). It turns out to be "as nothing," however, when compared with Solomon's awesome structure (2:3). Haggai, who has chided them, now encourages them. The people, currently poor, weak, and enslaved, will one day see the nations give God both wealth and glory in his house. All this began to happen in the coming of Jesus Christ and his worldwide gospel:

> Be strong, all you people of the land, declares the LORD. Work, for I am with you, declares the LORD of hosts, according to the covenant that I made with you when you came out of Egypt. My Spirit remains in your midst. Fear not. For thus says the LORD of hosts: Yet once more, in a little while, I will shake the heavens and the earth and the sea and the dry land. And I will shake all nations, so that the treasures of all nations shall come in, and I will fill this house with glory, says the LORD of hosts. The silver is mine, and the gold is mine, declares the LORD of hosts. The latter glory of this house shall be greater than the former, says the LORD of hosts. And in this place I will give peace, declares the LORD of hosts. (2:4–9)

Moreover, the covenantal curse is removed now (2:10–19), and one day Zerubbabel (or his descendant) will have royal authority over the nations (2:20–23).

38

Zechariah 8:23

*Thus says the LORD of hosts: In those days ten
men from the nations of every tongue shall take
hold of the robe of a Jew, saying, "Let us go with
you, for we have heard that God is with you."*

ZECHARIAH IS A CONTEMPORARY OF HAGGAI, THE PROPHET;
Zerubbabel, the governor; and Joshua, son of the high priest. The
temple has not yet been rebuilt, and the people who have returned
from exile are in physical misery and emotional exhaustion.
Dreams of a restored grandeur for Israel look like cruel delusions.
Many have "despised [this] day of small things" (Zech. 4:10).

Into the void steps Zechariah, calling on God's people to put
on their spiritual glasses and see reality for what it is. The first
part of the prophecy (1–8) presents a series of oracles and visions
urging the people, supposedly at the mercy of the gentile nations,
to repent and take heart as God works in their midst.[1]

- *Vision one* (1:7–17): The Lord's horsemen ask God to be
  merciful to Jerusalem.
- *Vision two* (1:18–21): Four horns and four craftsmen
  signify the chastening that the nations will receive for
  oppressing Israel.
- *Vision three* (2): The Lord will dwell in a secure Jerusalem
  without walls.

- *Vision four* (3): The Lord defends and cleanses Joshua, the high priest, and promises a "Branch" to purify and protect Israel.
- *Vision five* (4): The lampstand and the two olive trees signify the Lord's determination to help Zerubbabel and Joshua overcome all obstacles to rebuild the temple. But the work will be done "not by might, nor by power, but by my Spirit, says the LORD of hosts" (4:6).
- *Vision six* (5:1–4): The flying scroll represents the Lord's determination to punish those who break his covenant commandments.
- *Vision seven* (5:5–11): A woman in a basket symbolizes the people's wickedness being removed.
- *Vision eight* (6:1–8): Four chariots and their horses point to God's sovereignty in the world and his ultimate victory.
- *The action* (6:9–15): Joshua is crowned, pointing to success in rebuilding the temple.
- *The call* (7): The people are to act with both justice and mercy, not relying on heartless ritual obedience before God.
- *The blessing* (8): Israel, though lowly now in the eyes of the Gentiles, will, in fulfillment of the original promise to Abraham (Gen. 12:1–3), be blessed to be a blessing to the nations:

Thus says the LORD of hosts: Peoples shall yet come, even the inhabitants of many cities. The inhabitants of one city shall go to another, saying, "Let us go at once to entreat the favor of the LORD and to seek the LORD of hosts; I myself am going." Many peoples and strong nations shall come to seek the LORD of hosts in Jerusalem and to entreat the favor of the LORD. *Thus says the LORD of hosts: In those days ten men from the nations of every tongue shall take hold of the robe of a Jew, saying, "Let us go with you, for we have heard that God is with you."* (Zech. 8:20–23, emphasis added)

The book's second section (9–14) points to a coming King who will ultimately restore God's glory and the people's fortunes. Israel's enemies will face judgment (9:1–8) and the King will come:

> *Rejoice greatly, O daughter of Zion!*
> *Shout aloud, O daughter of Jerusalem!*
> *Behold, your king is coming to you;*
> *righteous and having salvation is he,*
> *humble and mounted on a donkey,*
> *on a colt, the foal of a donkey.* (9:9)

God will save his people (9:14–10:12), though Judah's worthless shepherds will be judged (11). Zechariah becomes a shepherd who is rejected by his people (11:12–13), prefiguring Christ's betrayal by Judas (Matt. 27:9–10). Ultimately, the Lord will be struck (Zech. 13:7) but will save his repentant people: "I will pour out on the house of David and the inhabitants of Jerusalem a spirit of grace and pleas for mercy, so that, when they look on me, on him whom they have pierced, they shall mourn for him, as one mourns for an only child, and weep bitterly over him, as one weeps over a firstborn" (12:10).

Yet the future is assured. A cataclysmic day of the Lord is coming (14:1–15), followed by the Lord's reign in Jerusalem (14:16–19), where even the bells of the horses will be inscribed with the words "Holy to the LORD" (14:20).

39

Malachi 1:11

*From the rising of the sun to its setting my
name will be great among the nations, and in
every place incense will be offered to my name,
and a pure offering. For my name will be great
among the nations, says the LORD of hosts.*

MALACHI, WHOSE NAME MEANS "MY MESSENGER," IS THE LAST OF
the Lord's Old Testament prophets. He is a contemporary of
Nehemiah, who rebuilt the walls of Jerusalem. In the book, God's
love for Israel is contrasted with the people's indifference—even
hatred—for him.

Malachi lays out a series of arguments between God and his
people. In each, God tells the truth about the current situation
(sometimes through piercing questions of his people), the people
or their leaders question what he says, and the Lord answers.

1:2–5:

STATEMENT: "I have loved you."
QUESTION: "How have you loved us?"
ANSWER: "I have loved Jacob but Esau I have hated."
God graciously chose his people out of love.

1:6–2:9:

QUESTIONS: "Where is my honor? . . . where is my fear? . . .
How have we despised your name?"
ANSWER: "By saying that the LORD's table may be despised."

In this exchange, the Lord reveals why it is so important for his people to honor him: *"My name will be great among the nations, and in every place incense will be offered to my name. . . . For my name will be great among the nations"* (1:11, emphasis added). "For I am a great King, says the LORD of hosts, and my name will be feared among the nations" (1:14). The Lord's goal is not to bless just Israel but through Israel to bless the world (Gen. 12:1–3).

2:10–16:

STATEMENT: "He no longer regards the offering or accepts it
with favor from your hand."
QUESTION: "Why does he not?"
ANSWER: "Because the LORD was witness between you
and the wife of your youth, to whom you have been
faithless." We cannot dichotomize our life obligations
into "religious" and "personal" realms. God requires
congruence to his character in both.

2:17–3:5:

STATEMENT: "You have wearied the LORD with your words."
QUESTION: "How have we wearied him?"
ANSWER: "By saying, 'Everyone who does evil is good in the
sight of the LORD, and he delights in them.' Or by asking,

'Where is the God of justice?'" (2:17). Amazingly, we weary the Lord by questioning his character.

3:6–12:

STATEMENTS: "Return to me, and I will return to you. . . . You are robbing me."

QUESTION: "How shall we return? . . . How have we robbed you?"

ANSWER: "In your tithes and contributions." Money is a key indicator of our hearts. As Jesus said, "You cannot serve God and money" (Matt. 6:24).

3:13–15:

STATEMENT: "Your words have been hard against me."

QUESTION: "How have we spoken against you?"

ANSWER: "You have said, 'It is vain to serve God. What is the profit of our keeping his charge or of walking as in mourning before the LORD of hosts? And now we call the arrogant blessed. Evildoers not only prosper but they put God to the test and they escape.'" If we serve God for the temporal benefits he sometimes graciously provides, we are missing the point. God has a bigger agenda.

We see glimpses of that agenda in Malachi. The bitter, grumbling people are told to prepare for the entrance of another "messenger, [who] will prepare the way before me. And the Lord whom you seek will suddenly come to his temple; and the messenger of the covenant in whom you delight, behold, he is coming, says the LORD of hosts" (3:1).

Moreover, judgment is ahead for "all the arrogant and all

evildoers" (4:1), so it is time to repent. The God of justice is coming, and he will make a distinction between those who love him and those who don't: "For you who fear my name, the sun of righteousness shall rise with healing in its wings. You shall go out leaping like calves from the stall. And you shall tread down the wicked, for they will be ashes under the soles of your feet, on the day when I act, says the LORD of hosts" (4:2–3).

That day will be preceded by the coming of "Elijah," who will "turn the hearts of fathers to their children and the hearts of children to their fathers" (4:5–6). God requires right actions, of course, but he graciously provides the spiritual power to obey him. Christians, of course, see the messenger (Elijah) as John the Baptist (Matt. 11:10–14) and Jesus as the promised Lord, who came once in mercy to die for the sins of the world (Mark 10:45) and who will come again in judgment (Matt. 3:1–11), making his name great among the nations.

NEW TESTAMENT

40

Matthew 16:15

He said to them, "But who do you say that I am?"

THE OLD TESTAMENT SURELY IS ONE OF THE MOST TRAGIC BOOKS in all of literature. It begins with a majestic Creator who graciously sets a man and a woman in a garden. They rebel against his loving, kingly rule, however, and are expelled from his presence, setting in motion a devastating series of events that culminates in a global deluge. God begins again, with Abraham, seeking to establish a righteous people who will draw the nations to himself, under the royal line of David.

But despite nearly countless displays of the holy Lord's patient faithfulness, the people of Israel rebel and face his judgment—expulsion from the promised land. By his grace, a chastened remnant eventually returns, looking for God to fulfill his promises of a coming King and kingdom. The glory days are past, however. Israel is now subject to one pagan empire after another, its pivotal role in the divine plan seemingly over.

Matthew tells the story of how God intervenes personally, continuing the divine plan in a way that his people never expected. Matthew, one of four ancient biographies in the New Testament called the Gospels, begins with "Jesus Christ, the son of David, the son of Abraham" (1:1). An angel tells Joseph, Christ's earthly father, that Jesus "will save his people from their sins" (1:21). Magi from the East see his star and ask, "Where is he who has been born king of the Jews?" (2:2).

Acknowledgment of Jesus' royal identity is far from universal in Israel, however. Herod, the illegitimate king, tries to kill him (2:16–18). When Jesus teaches with divine authority, using the formula "You have heard that it was said. . . . But I say to you" (5:21–22, 27–28), the people are "astonished at his teaching, for he was teaching them as one who had authority, and not as their scribes" (7:28–29).

When Jesus miraculously asserts his authority over the elements, his disciples ask, "What sort of man is this, that even winds and sea obey him?" (8:27). Even Christ's messenger, John the Baptist, asks, "Are you the one who is to come, or shall we look for another?" (11:3). Several cities snub him (11:20–24). The Pharisees reject his miracles and seek to destroy him (12:14–45). Yet Jesus' royal identity is the paramount issue. One day he asks his disciples, *"But who do you say that I am?"* (16:15, emphasis added).

Evidence of Christ's kingship is evident in his teaching. The book presents five discourses, parallels to the five books of Moses, Israel's first lawgiver:

5–7: THE KING'S PEOPLE: "Blessed are the poor in spirit, for theirs is the kingdom of heaven" (5:3).

10: THE KING'S MESSENGERS: "Behold, I am sending you out as sheep in the midst of wolves, so be wise as serpents and innocent as doves" (10:16).

13: THE KING'S PARABLES: "To you it has been given to know the secrets of the kingdom of heaven, but to them it has not been given" (13:11).

18: THE KING'S CHURCH: "Who is the greatest in the kingdom of heaven?" (18:1).

24–25: THE KING'S RETURN: "When the Son of Man comes

in his glory, and all the angels with him, then he will sit on his glorious throne. Before him will be gathered all the nations, and he will separate people one from another as a shepherd separates the sheep from the goats" (25:31–32).

For now, however, Christ has come in humility, and most of his people reject him (26), sending him to the cross (27). But soon tragedy turns to triumph. On the third day, Jesus rises from the grave as the royal Son of God, receiving the worship of his surprised disciples (28:1–17). Then the King sends his servants on a royal, global mission: "All authority in heaven and on earth has been given to me. Go therefore and make disciples of all nations, baptizing them in the name of the Father and of the Son and of the Holy Spirit, teaching them to observe all that I have commanded you. And behold, I am with you always, to the end of the age" (28:18–20).

The promises of the Old Testament are being fulfilled, both now and ultimately, in Jesus Christ the King.

41

Mark 10:45

*Even the Son of Man came not to be served but to
serve, and to give his life as a ransom for many.*

MARK BEGINS WITH THE WORDS, "THE BEGINNING OF THE GOSPEL
of Jesus Christ, the Son of God" (1:1). Jesus explodes across the
pages of this brief but action-packed thriller. "More than any
other Gospel," Mark Dever writes,

> Mark highlights action over teaching, which leaves us with the
> impression of a dramatic story. Mark's favorite word is *euthus*,
> which means "straightway" or "immediately." . . . "And imme-
> diately, they left their nets . . ." (1:18); "And immediately, he
> called them . . ." (1:20); "And immediately . . . he entered . . ."
> (1:21); "And immediately there was . . ." (1:23). Again and
> again, he cuts to a different camera shot.[1]

Jesus' many actions demonstrate his authority[2] over the
following: human priorities and traditions (1:14–20; 2:13–17;
2:23–28; 3:31–35; 4:1–34; 7:1–30); the elements (4:35–41; 6:30–
52; 8:1–10); disease and disability (1:29–34; 1:40–2:12; 5:21–43;
6:53–56; 7:31–37; 8:22–26); and the demonic (1:21–28; 3:7–12;
5:1–20). When demons cry out in shock, "You are the Son of God,"
Jesus even orders them to be quiet (3:11–12). Yet his authority can
be rejected or misunderstood (5:1–12; 6:51; 8:11–21).

The book is not all "show" and no "tell," however. At the mid-point, the authoritative Jesus asks his disciples (as in the gospel of Matthew) if they know his identity. Peter says he is the Christ, and Jesus again commands silence on the matter (8:27–30). But he quickly starts overturning their expectations of what a Messiah is supposed to be and do:

> He began to teach them that the Son of Man must suffer many things and be rejected by the elders and the chief priests and the scribes and be killed, and after three days rise again. (8:31)

> If anyone would come after me, let him deny himself and take up his cross and follow me. For whoever would save his life will lose it, but whoever loses his life for my sake and the gospel's will save it. For what does it profit a man to gain the whole world and forfeit his soul? For what can a man give in return for his soul? For whoever is ashamed of me and of my words in this adulterous and sinful generation, of him will the Son of Man also be ashamed when he comes in the glory of his Father with the holy angels. (8:34–38)

> How is it written of the Son of Man that he should suffer many things and be treated with contempt? (9:12)

> The Son of Man is going to be delivered into the hands of men, and they will kill him. And when he is killed, after three days he will rise. (9:31)

> See, we are going up to Jerusalem, and the Son of Man will be delivered over to the chief priests and the scribes, and they will condemn him to death and deliver him over to the Gentiles. And they will mock him and spit on him, and flog him and kill him. And after three days he will rise. (10:33–34)

Despite all these warnings, two disciples, James and John, ask to be seated at his side when he inaugurates the kingdom (10:35–37). Jesus answers by contrasting earthly authority with kingdom authority:

> You know that those who are considered rulers of the Gentiles lord it over them, and their great ones exercise authority over them. But it shall not be so among you. But whoever would be great among you must be your servant, and whoever would be first among you must be slave of all. *For even the Son of Man came not to be served but to serve, and to give his life as a ransom for many.* (10:42–45, emphasis added)

The rest of Mark shows Jesus doing just that—serving humanity by going to Jerusalem, giving up his life, and rising on the third day (11–12; 14–16). Yet one day Jesus Christ, the Son of God, says he will act not as Servant but as the authoritative Master of the universe:

> In those days, after that tribulation, the sun will be darkened, and the moon will not give its light, and the stars will be falling from heaven, and the powers in the heavens will be shaken. And then they will see the Son of Man coming in clouds with great power and glory. And then he will send out the angels and gather his elect from the four winds, from the ends of the earth to the ends of heaven. (13:24–27)

Those who have refused Christ's service to their souls, who have rejected the ransom for their freedom bought at Calvary, will one day have to explain why to the Son of Man, who is coming again.

42

Luke 4:18

The Spirit of the Lord is upon me,
because he has anointed me
to proclaim good news to the poor.
He has sent me to proclaim liberty to the captives
and recovering of sight to the blind,
to set at liberty those who are oppressed.

THIS GOSPEL IS BELIEVED TO BE WRITTEN BY LUKE, THE "BELOVED physician" and gentile traveling companion of Paul (Col. 4:14). The biography that today bears Luke's name—concerning "all that Jesus began to do and teach, until the day when he was taken up" (Acts 1:1–2)—is the first part of a narrative that continues with Acts, which covers the creation and growth of the church. As the key verse says, Luke portrays the Holy Spirit, gospel proclamation, and physical and spiritual freedom for the oppressed as indispensable elements in the ministry of Jesus, the Messiah for both Jew and Gentile.

Jesus describes his ministry by pointing back to Isaiah 61:1–2, which speaks most immediately to the people's release from Babylonian exile, and to Isaiah 42:1, 7, which says that the mission of God's coming "servant" is "to open the eyes that are blind." Jesus says his mission is to free those imprisoned in physical and spiritual darkness.

Luke is replete with power encounters on behalf of the captive and oppressed: a man with leprosy (5:12–16); a man who was paralyzed (5:17–26); a man with a withered hand (6:6–11); a formerly dead son (7:11–17); a demon-afflicted man (8:26–39); a woman with a long-term discharge of blood (8:43–48); and a child who has died (8:49–55). Jesus proclaims his good news to the "poor" (6:20), those who know their spiritual poverty and frequently come to him with physical needs as well:

Depart from me, for I am a sinful man, O Lord. (5:8)

Great crowds gathered to hear him and to be healed of their infirmities. (5:15)

"That you may know that the Son of Man has authority on earth to forgive sins"—he said to the man who was paralyzed—"I say to you, rise, pick up your bed and go home." (5:24)

Those who are well have no need of a physician, but those who are sick. I have not come to call the righteous but sinners to repentance. (5:31–32)

The Holy Spirit, the third person of the Trinity, is prominent in Jesus' life and ministry (3:16; 5:17). He is also seen powerfully working in John the Baptist (1:15), in Simeon (2:25–27), and in the coming ministry of Christ's followers (24:49). What Jesus does, he does in the power of the Holy Spirit, and his disciples have available that same Spirit and power (11:19–20).

Luke takes special note of God's concern for the world as demonstrated in the life, death, and resurrection of Christ. "Glory to God in the highest," the angels proclaim at the Lord's birth, "and on earth peace among those with whom he is pleased!" (2:14). God's peace is *offered* not just to the faithful in Israel but to anyone willing to trust and obey (7:1–10; 9:51–56; 10:25–36; 16:8).

God's peace, however, is not *given* to everyone. "Do you think that I have come to give peace on earth?" Jesus asks. "No, I tell you, but rather division" (12:51). The consequences of such a terrible rejection of Jesus' good news are everlasting. "In that place there will be weeping and gnashing of teeth, when you see Abraham and Isaac and Jacob and all the prophets in the kingdom of God but you yourselves cast out," Jesus says to some hard-hearted Jewish leaders. "And people will come from east and west, and from north and south, and recline at table in the kingdom of God. And behold, some are last who will be first, and some are first who will be last" (13:28–30).

Jesus forgives those who crucify him, including the Roman soldiers (23:34). A centurion, unlike the leading Jews, proclaims him innocent (23:47). And when Jesus has risen from the dead, he gives his disciples their global marching orders:

> Thus it is written, that the Christ should suffer and on the third day rise from the dead, and that repentance and forgiveness of sins should be proclaimed in his name to all nations, beginning from Jerusalem. You are witnesses of these things. And behold, I am sending the promise of my Father upon you. But stay in the city until you are clothed with power from on high. (24:46–49)

The God-given, global ministry of physical and spiritual freedom that Christ inaugurated in the power of the Spirit will continue in the lives of his faithful followers until Jesus returns.

43

John 1:14

The Word became flesh and dwelt among us, and
we have seen his glory, glory as of the only Son
from the Father, full of grace and truth.

THE GOSPEL OF MATTHEW BEGINS WITH A GENEALOGY LINKING Jesus to Abraham, the father of the Jewish nation. Mark starts his account of Christ with the ministry of John the Baptist. Luke begins with the birth narratives of the Baptist and Jesus. John, however, goes back to the beginning—the *very* beginning. Echoing Genesis, he writes, "In the beginning was the Word, and the Word was with God, and the Word was God. He was in the beginning with God. All things were made through him, and without him was not any thing made that was made. In him was life, and the life was the light of men" (1:1–4). This Word of God called the universe into existence: "God said, 'Let there be light,' and there was light" (Gen. 1:3).

And yet John says that the divine Word, a person, was rejected by many on earth: "He came to his own, and his own people did not receive him" (1:11). But not all: "But to all who did receive him, who believed in his name, he gave the right to become children of God, who were born, not of blood nor of the will of the flesh nor of the will of man, but of God" (1:12–13). In the key verse, John describes into which group *he* falls: "The

Word became flesh and dwelt among us, and we have seen his glory, glory as of the only Son from the Father, full of grace and truth" (1:14).

The Word became flesh. Jesus discloses himself as the God-man, fully divine and fully human, finding faith in some and unbelief in others: "This was why the Jews were seeking all the more to kill him, because not only was he breaking the Sabbath, but he was even calling God his own Father, making himself equal with God" (5:18).

And dwelt among us. He was *sent*: "God did not send his Son into the world to condemn the world, but in order that the world might be saved through him" (3:17).

We have seen his glory, glory as of the only Son from the Father. He who has seen Jesus has seen the Father (14:9). The Son does what the Father does: "Truly, truly, I say to you, the Son can do nothing of his own accord, but only what he sees the Father doing. . . . For as the Father raises the dead and gives them life, so also the Son gives life to whom he will. The Father judges no one, but has given all judgment to the Son, that all may honor the Son, just as they honor the Father" (5:19–23).

Full of grace and truth. Jesus speaks God's truth, which can hurt, but he also shares God's grace. We see this in his tender but uncompromising treatment of a sinful but searching woman of Samaria:

> Many Samaritans from that town believed in him because of the woman's testimony, "He told me all that I ever did." So . . . they asked him to stay with them, and he stayed there two days. And many more believed because of his word. They said to the woman, "It is no longer because of what you said that we believe . . . we know that this is indeed the Savior of the world." (4:39–42)

Chapters 2–11 present seven signs[1] that reveal the Son of God: turning water into wine at the wedding in Cana (2:1–11); cleansing the temple (2:13–22); healing an official's son (4:46–54); healing a lame man at the Bethesda pool (5:1–15); feeding the five thousand (6:1–15); healing a man born blind (9); and raising Jesus' friend Lazarus from the dead (11:1–44).

Chapter 12 transitions into the final phase of Jesus' ministry of grace and truth—his farewell to the disciples (13–17), his death (18–19), his resurrection (20), and his instructions to Peter and John (21). John the evangelist tells us his motivation in writing the book—to help others see the grace and truth of the Word and receive him as their Savior, thereby becoming his spiritual children: "Now Jesus did many other signs in the presence of the disciples, which are not written in this book; but these are written so that you may believe that Jesus is the Christ, the Son of God, and that by believing you may have life in his name" (20:30–31).

John calls on his readers—*us*—to believe in Jesus in order to partake of the grace and truth still available today.

44

Acts 1:8

You will receive power when the Holy Spirit has come
upon you, and you will be my witnesses in Jerusalem and
in all Judea and Samaria, and to the end of the earth.

LUKE'S STORY OF "ALL THAT JESUS BEGAN TO DO" CONTINUES IN
the book of Acts (1:1). While Jesus appears, often with instructions, at key moments (1:1–11; 9:1–22; 10:1–16; 19:11–20), the
apostles and their successors take center stage in the global expansion of his church. Our key verse points out that they do this in the
power of the Spirit.

You will receive power when the Holy Spirit has come upon you.
Formerly mostly in the background as God's saving plan for the
world has unfolded, now the Spirit, described as "the promise of
my Father" (Luke 24:49), is present with power for the disciples
at critical inflection points: the founding of the church (Acts 2);
the preaching of Stephen (6:5–7:55); the preaching of Philip in
Samaria and with an Ethiopian eunuch (8:12–25, 29); the filling
and healing of Saul (9:17); the conversion of the Gentiles (10:44–
45; 11:15); the ordination of Saul (later, Paul) and Barnabas for
the first missionary journey (13:4–10); and the conversion of the
Gentiles (13:52).

And you will be my witnesses in Jerusalem. The disciples begin
in Jerusalem, the capital of the Jewish nation. In the City of

David, the disciples choose a successor to Judas (1:12–26); are empowered by the Spirit (2:1–13); preach to the Jewish people (2:14–41); model Christian community (2:42–47); preach, heal, and pray (3–4); purify the movement (5:1–11); continue their witness and suffer for it (5:12–42); name deacons (6:1–7); and preach and face even more persecution (7:1–8:3). The Jerusalem church remains a key influence in the growth of God's people and the inclusion of the Gentiles (15).

And in all Judea and Samaria. The gospel spreads in the geographical regions near Jerusalem, among Jews and Samaritans (8:4–24), as well as among God-fearing Gentiles such as Cornelius (10). Paul is converted from a Christian hater to a risk-taking apostle (9); Peter publicly welcomes Gentiles as fellow believers (11:1–18).

And to the end of the earth. The great church in Antioch is founded, sending Paul and Barnabas to help the saints in Jerusalem (11:19–30; 12:25); James is killed and Peter is spared (12:1–19); and Herod Agrippa, a persecutor of the church, is judged (12:19–24). With the support of the church in Antioch (13:1–3), Paul and Barnabas go on the first missionary journey (13–14). They spread the gospel in Cyprus and southern Asia Minor. They speak to Romans (13:4–12), Jews scattered across the empire (13:13–51), and uneducated pagan worshipers of Zeus and Hermes (14:8–18). Opposition at times is fierce (13:50–52; 14:19–22), but churches of faithful disciples are established (14:23–28).

Then Paul and Barnabas separate over John Mark, the author of the second gospel, so Barnabas returns to Cyprus (15:36–39) while Paul takes other helpers, Silas and Timothy, on his second missionary journey to Macedonia and Achaia (15:40–18:23). This journey opens Europe to the gospel (16:6–10). A well-to-do woman, Lydia, is Paul's first convert there (16:11–15). Paul and Silas upset the local slave trade and are thrown in prison

(16:16–24), where the Lord delivers them spectacularly, bringing the jailer and his family to saving faith (16:25–40).

Paul preaches his famous sermon at the Areopagus in Athens (17:16–34), proclaiming to the pagan religious elites, "The times of ignorance God overlooked, but now he commands all people everywhere to repent, because he has fixed a day on which he will judge the world in righteousness by a man whom he has appointed; and of this he has given assurance to all by raising him from the dead" (17:30–31). The gospel is for everyone on earth.

Paul's third missionary journey (18:23–21:16) occurs mostly in Ephesus, the commercial capital of the Roman province of Asia.[1] As his ministry winds down, Paul tells the new believers there that he has been called back to Jerusalem, "constrained by the Spirit, not knowing what will happen to me there, except that the Holy Spirit testifies to me in every city that imprisonment and afflictions await me" (20:22–23).

And indeed such troubles come to Paul. He is arrested in Jerusalem (21:17–23:35); preaches in Caesarea (24–26); and goes to Rome (27–28). Paul survives an assassination plot, religious indifference, political manipulation and intrigue, shipwreck, and a poisonous viper bite. Yet even under Roman house arrest, where the book abruptly ends, Paul has the freedom to teach "about the Lord Jesus Christ with all boldness and without hindrance" (28:31).

The worldwide work of Christ's witnesses, done in the power of the Spirit, goes on.

45

Romans 1:16

*I am not ashamed of the gospel, for it is the power
of God for salvation to everyone who believes,
to the Jew first and also to the Greek.*

PAUL IS WINDING DOWN HIS THIRD MISSIONARY JOURNEY, HAVING
spread the good news in Judea, Asia Minor, and parts of Europe. He
hopes next to preach the gospel in Rome, the strategic seat of secular power and site of a church consisting of Jew and Gentile alike.
But what is the gospel, and how do Israelites and non-Israelites unite
under its banner? The apostle answers these questions in the grand
theological (yet practical) treatise known as Romans.

Introducing himself to these believers, Paul puts the gospel
in context, calling himself "an apostle, set apart for the gospel
of God, which he promised beforehand through his prophets
in the holy Scriptures, concerning his Son, who was descended
from David according to the flesh" (1:1–3). The gospel, or good
news, that Paul preaches was predicted in the Old Testament and
centers on Jesus Christ, the Messiah. And it is for all. "I am not
ashamed of the gospel," the key verse says, "for it is the power of
God for salvation to everyone who believes, to the Jew first and
also to the Greek" (1:16).

Then Paul describes the gospel's key elements: "In it the righteousness of God is revealed from faith for faith, as it is written,

'The righteous shall live by faith'" (1:17). Our salvation, given through God's power, is all about righteousness, faith, and life. It is good news indeed.

But having outlined the good news, Paul must then give us the bad. "The wrath of God," Paul writes, "is revealed from heaven against all ungodliness and unrighteousness of men, who by their unrighteousness suppress the truth" (1:18). We need the gospel because of God's righteous wrath against the unrighteousness of mankind apart from him. The verse is reminiscent of Jesus' words in John 3:18: "Whoever believes in him is not condemned, but whoever does not believe is condemned already."

In the following section (Rom. 1:18–3:20), the apostle proves that both Jew and Gentile stand guilty before God. The Gentiles have rejected the light they had, while the Jews have failed to obey the law God gave. "By works of the law no human being will be justified in his sight," Paul says (3:20). The gospel is needed because "all have sinned and fall short of the glory of God" (3:23).

Paul describes (3:21–4:25) the good news of how sinful humanity can be made righteous in God's eyes. Right standing with God comes through Christ's "propitiation by his blood, to be received by faith" (3:25). On the cross, Jesus took the wrath we deserve, allowing God to be "just and the justifier of the one who has faith in Jesus" (3:26). Answering the objection of some that the Old Testament does not teach justification by faith, Paul points to Abraham (and to Gen. 15:6, the first key verse in this book), who "believed God, and it was counted to him as righteousness" (4:3).

Such belief averts God's wrath, leading to peace with him (5) and power over personal sin, even though holy living remains a struggle (6:1–8:17). It also points to glory in the future (8:18–22), which helps us be patient in the meantime: "We know that for those who love God all things work together for good" (8:28).

Given all this good news, then, why have the Jewish people

rejected their Messiah (9–11)? Paul freely admits to "great sorrow and unceasing anguish" for his countrymen (9:2). He says that the current overall Jewish response to Jesus fits the Old Testament pattern of God's choice of "children of the promise" over "children of the flesh" (9:8) and that righteousness always comes by faith (9:6–29).

Yet the gospel is for *all*: "There is no distinction between Jew and Greek; for the same Lord is Lord of all, bestowing his riches on all who call on him" (10:12). Jews and Gentiles are and will be members of the same community of belief (11).

In view of all this good news, believers are called to live righteously for God today—loving one another, submitting to the authorities, and following the example of Christ (12:1–16:27). "I appeal to you therefore, brothers," Paul says, "by the mercies of God, to present your bodies as a living sacrifice, holy and acceptable to God, which is your spiritual worship. Do not be conformed to this world, but be transformed by the renewal of your mind, that by testing you may discern what is the will of God, what is good and acceptable and perfect" (12:1–2).

The gospel is for all, today and tomorrow.

46

1 Corinthians 12:13

*In one Spirit we were all baptized into one
body—Jews or Greeks, slaves or free—
and all were made to drink of one Spirit.*

PEOPLE OFTEN COMPLAIN ABOUT ALL THE HYPOCRITES IN THE church—those who fail to practice what they preach. It is a problem as old as the church itself.[1] The church in Corinth might be Exhibit A. Judging from the issues Paul addresses in 1 Corinthians, the believers in this prosperous city, whom Paul acknowledges are gifted, have no qualms about living like pagans.

Their first problem is disunity. "I appeal to you, brothers," Paul writes, "by the name of our Lord Jesus Christ, that all of you agree, and that there be no divisions among you, but that you be united in the same mind and the same judgment. For it has been reported to me by Chloe's people that there is quarreling among you, my brothers" (1:10–11).

The disunity grows out of worldly standards concerning the eloquence and wisdom of various preachers who have come through the city (1:10–4:21). Paul reminds the church that the gospel is not based on supposed human wisdom:

> The word of the cross is folly to those who are perishing, but to us who are being saved it is the power of God. For it is written,

"I will destroy the wisdom of the wise,
> and the discernment of the discerning I will thwart."
(1:18–19)

The people are proud of what they know and what they can do. Paul says that pride is not a Christian virtue:

Consider your calling, brothers: not many of you were wise according to worldly standards, not many were powerful, not many were of noble birth. But God chose what is foolish in the world to shame the wise; God chose what is weak in the world to shame the strong; God chose what is low and despised in the world, even things that are not, to bring to nothing things that are, so that no human being might boast in the presence of God. (1:26–29)

Much of this letter addresses the problems and questions in the fellowship in Corinth. The church allows both sexual immorality—even incest—and a culture in which Christians sue one another (5–6). Members wonder what to do about marriage, divorce, and chastity (7); question whether it is all right to eat food sacrificed to pagan idols (8); and misunderstand the connection between the resurrection of Christ and their own (15). Their corporate worship is unruly and unloving (11), and they even compete against one another in the gifts provided by God for the good of the church (12; 14).

Paul takes two lines of argument to bring the Corinthians to their senses. First, he reminds them that they are *one body*. Thus, they must work for the common good. The key verse, if received with humility, is a powerful antidote to the poisonous disease of selfishness and division running rampant in the Corinthian church and in our own: "Just as the body is one and has many members, and all the members of the body, though many, are one body, so it is with Christ. *For in one Spirit we were all baptized into one body—Jews or Greeks, slaves or free—and all were made to drink of one Spirit"* (12:12–13, emphasis added).

Second, Paul says, the unity of all believers—produced by the Holy Spirit at our conversion—must result in spiritual actions and attitudes. We must *love*, Paul says, echoing the command of the Lord, who told the disciples the night he was betrayed: "A new commandment I give to you, that you love one another: just as I have loved you, you also are to love one another" (John 13:34). Paul explains,

> If I speak in the tongues of men and of angels, but have not love, I am a noisy gong or a clanging cymbal. And if I have prophetic powers, and understand all mysteries and all knowledge, and if I have all faith, so as to remove mountains, but have not love, I am nothing. If I give away all I have, and if I deliver up my body to be burned, but have not love, I gain nothing.
>
> Love is patient and kind; love does not envy or boast; it is not arrogant or rude. It does not insist on its own way; it is not irritable or resentful; it does not rejoice at wrongdoing, but rejoices with the truth. Love bears all things, believes all things, hopes all things, endures all things. (1 Cor. 13:1–7)

The apostle John echoes the thought: "Beloved, let us love one another, for love is from God, and whoever loves has been born of God and knows God" (1 John 4:7).

Paul says that a healthy body—whether in the physical or the spiritual realm—will not war against itself. And it begins in the heart.

47

2 Corinthians 4:7

We have this treasure in jars of clay, to show that the
surpassing power belongs to God and not to us.

IT IS A YEAR AFTER THE WRITING OF 1 CORINTHIANS. PAUL, IN MACEDONIA, has heard that many in the fractious Corinthian church are questioning his apostleship and even his honesty because he had to change his plans, has faced tremendous obstacles in his life and ministry, and now is asking for money for the suffering church in Jerusalem.[1] The first seven chapters of this letter are a defense of his apostleship; chapters 8–9 appeal to the church to give generously to the saints in Jerusalem; and chapters 10–13 attempt to win over those who still question him and his ministry.

Paul zealously defends his ministry because to reject it is to reject Christ himself. Freely admitting that his plans had changed, Paul nevertheless claims the leading of God in his apostleship:

> Thanks be to God, who in Christ always leads us in triumphal procession, and through us spreads the fragrance of the knowledge of him everywhere. For we are the aroma of Christ to God among those who are being saved and among those who are perishing, to one a fragrance from death to death, to the other a fragrance from life to life. (2:14–16)

Paul says that his struggles, rather than being disqualifiers, confirm that God is working through him and qualify him to comfort others as a minister of the new and better covenant. "Blessed be the God and Father of our Lord Jesus Christ, the Father of mercies and God of all comfort," Paul writes, "who comforts us in all our affliction, so that we may be able to comfort those who are in any affliction, with the comfort with which we ourselves are comforted by God" (1:3–4).

"Therefore," Paul says, "having this ministry by the mercy of God, we do not lose heart" (4:1). The focus is "not ourselves, but Jesus Christ as Lord, with ourselves as your servants for Jesus' sake" (4:5). Thus, it is only natural that Paul—and any minister of the gospel—is a weak vessel, so that what he carries, the message of salvation, should stand out all the more, as the key verse indicates: "We have this treasure in jars of clay, to show that the surpassing power belongs to God and not to us" (4:7).

That treasure includes the promise to believers of a coming "heavenly dwelling" (physical resurrection), with the present indwelling "Spirit as a guarantee" of what is to come (5:1–5). Yet we must be ready. Christ will judge his people: "We must all appear before the judgment seat of Christ, so that each one may receive what is due for what he has done in the body, whether good or evil" (5:10). That's why the apostle carries on with the awesome ministry of reconciliation:

> Therefore, knowing the fear of the Lord, we persuade others. . . . For the love of Christ controls us, because we have concluded this: that one has died for all . . . that those who live might no longer live for themselves but for him who for their sake died and was raised.
>
> . . . Therefore, if anyone is in Christ, he is a new creation. The old has passed away; behold, the new has come. All

this is from God, who through Christ reconciled us to himself and gave us the ministry of reconciliation. . . . Therefore, we are ambassadors for Christ, God making his appeal through us. (5:11–20)

Stating his love once again for the Corinthians (6–7), Paul encourages them to prepare their previously promised offering for the believers in Jerusalem (8–9). He writes, "As you excel in everything—in faith, in speech, in knowledge, in all earnestness, and in our love for you—see that you excel in this act of grace also" (8:7).

Closing this letter, Paul returns to the theme of his weakness as a paradoxical sign of the Lord's presence. The apostle says that he asked the Lord three times to remove an unspecified "thorn" in the flesh:

He said to me, "My grace is sufficient for you, for my power is made perfect in weakness." Therefore I will boast all the more gladly of my weaknesses, so that the power of Christ may rest upon me. For the sake of Christ, then, I am content with weaknesses, insults, hardships, persecutions, and calamities. For when I am weak, then I am strong. (12:9–10)

It is the only logical choice for a jar of clay.

48

Galatians 2:16

We know that a person is not justified by works of
the law but through faith in Jesus Christ, so we also
have believed in Christ Jesus, in order to be justified
by faith in Christ and not by works of the law,
because by works of the law no one will be justified.

PAUL HAS SUCH A STRONG RELATIONSHIP WITH MEMBERS OF THE
church he started in Galatia that he can tell them the truth, even
if it hurts:

> I am astonished that you are so quickly deserting him who
> called you in the grace of Christ and are turning to a differ-
> ent gospel—not that there is another one, but there are some
> who trouble you and want to distort the gospel of Christ. But
> even if we or an angel from heaven should preach to you a
> gospel contrary to the one we preached to you, let him be
> accursed. (1:6–8)

"O foolish Galatians!" he says with concern bordering on
frustration (3:1). "Who has bewitched you?" Before respond-
ing to this different, distorted gospel, the apostle reminds the
Galatians of his credentials. He is

- "an apostle—not from men nor through man, but through Jesus Christ and God the Father" (1:1);
- "a servant of Christ" (1:10);
- "set . . . apart before I was born . . . called . . . by his grace" (1:15);
- "entrusted with the gospel to the uncircumcised" (2:7);
- equal to the other apostles (1:16–2:9); and
- consistent enough to stand up to Peter's former hypocrisy (2:11–14).

The "different gospel" the Galatians were embracing held that the Spirit is received at the beginning of the Christian life "by works of the law" rather than "hearing with faith," that we are "perfected by the flesh" (human effort) rather than "by the Spirit," and that the Spirit works and miracles come by human effort rather than faith (3:1–5). In other words, their distorted gospel said that justification (being made right with God) and sanctification (living a life of increasing holiness) come from human work rather than faith and the Spirit.

This is anathema to Paul, who reminds them that Jesus was crucified (3:1). In no uncertain terms, he lays out the choice for the Galatians and all who would follow: *We know that a person is not justified by works of the law but through faith in Jesus Christ, so we also have believed in Christ Jesus, in order to be justified by faith in Christ and not by works of the law, because by works of the law no one will be justified* (2:16, emphasis added). Three times in this key verse he says that justification comes *not* from works; two times he says it comes *by* faith.

To make his point, Paul says that justification by faith, not works, is from the Old Testament, referring to Genesis 15:6 (our book's first key verse)—"Abraham 'believed God, and it was counted to him as righteousness'" (Gal. 3:6)—before adding:

Know then that it is those of faith who are the sons of Abraham. And the Scripture, foreseeing that God would justify the Gentiles by faith, preached the gospel beforehand to Abraham, saying, "In you shall all the nations be blessed." So then, those who are of faith are blessed along with Abraham, the man of faith. (Gal. 3:7–9)

Then the apostle marshals his evidence. He draws a distinction between faith and the law, saying that, as Habakkuk said, "The righteous shall live by faith" (3:11–14). The law was an interlude of necessity between the covenant given to Abraham and the promised coming of Christ. He calls the law "our guardian until Christ came" (3:15–24). Now that faith has come, the guardian is no longer needed. We are all "sons of God, through faith," and all human distinctions fade next to our identity as Christians, "heirs according to promise" (3:26–29).

Paul then contrasts the freedom of faith with the slavery of being under the law, noting that the Galatians are children of promise. There can be no mixing of the two (4).

Finally, Paul tells believers to reject circumcision as a sign of acceptance before God. "For freedom Christ has set us free," Paul says, "stand firm therefore, and do not submit again to a yoke of slavery" (5:1). Those who do are "obligated to keep the whole law ... [and] have fallen away from grace" (5:1–4). Those who walk by the Spirit, however, can fulfill "the whole law" by obeying the command: "You shall love your neighbor as yourself" (5:5–14).

Such love mixes good works (6:1–10) and good but hard words (6:11–18). But being right with God is worth it.

49

Ephesians 2:8

By grace you have been saved through faith. And
this is not your own doing; it is the gift of God.

EPHESIANS, UNLIKE OTHER NEW TESTAMENT LETTERS FROM PAUL, addresses no problems in the church. The first of the Prison Epistles, it focuses on the blessings that believers have in Christ by the grace of God (1–3) and their practical implications (4–6).

Paul lists many of these blessings: "blessed us in Christ with every spiritual blessing in the heavenly places"; "predestined us for adoption as sons"; "redemption through his blood, the forgiveness of our trespasses"; "his grace . . . lavished upon us"; "obtained an inheritance"; and "sealed with the promised Holy Spirit, who is the guarantee of our inheritance" (1:3–14).

Given all this, Paul gives thanks for the Ephesians, praying that they may receive "the Spirit of wisdom and of revelation in the knowledge of him" and "may know what is the hope to which he has called you, what are the riches of his glorious inheritance in the saints, and what is the immeasurable greatness of his power toward us who believe" (1:15–19). Paul prays that they will understand all that God has done for them.

To drive home the point, he contrasts their state before Christ—"dead in the trespasses and sins . . . following the course of this world, following the prince of the power of the air . . . in

164

the passions of our flesh ... by nature children of wrath" (2:1–3)—with their redeemed state "by grace" (2:5). The result is that believers have been "raised ... up with him and seated ... in the heavenly places" (2:6). In the future, God will "show the immeasurable riches of his grace in kindness toward us in Christ Jesus" (2:7). Summing it all up, Paul adds, *"By grace you have been saved through faith. And this is not your own doing; it is the gift of God,* not a result of works, so that no one may boast" (2:8–9, emphasis added).

God's unmerited favor has implications for believers. The first is the reality of unity between Jew and Gentile (2:11–3:20). "He himself is our peace," Paul reminds them, "who has made us both one and has broken down in his flesh the dividing wall of hostility ... that he might create in himself one new man in place of the two, so making peace" (2:14–15).

This spiritual reality must find practical expression in the church. "I therefore," Paul writes, "... urge you to walk in a manner worthy of the calling to which you have been called, with all humility and gentleness, with patience, bearing with one another in love, eager to maintain the unity of the Spirit in the bond of peace" (4:1–3).

We are also to be holy. Paul says, "Let each one of you speak the truth with his neighbor, for we are members one of another. Be angry and do not sin.... Let the thief no longer steal, but rather let him labor, doing honest work with his own hands, so that he may have something to share with anyone in need. Let no corrupting talk come out of your mouths" (4:25–29). We are to "be imitators of God, as beloved children. And walk in love, as Christ loved us and gave himself up for us" (5:1–2).

"Look carefully then how you walk," Paul advises, "not as unwise but as wise, making the best use of the time, because the days are evil" (5:15–16), "submitting to one another out of reverence for Christ" (5:21). This churchly picture of humility extends to the Christian home.

Wives are to "submit to your own husbands, as to the Lord" (5:22). Husbands must "love your wives, as Christ loved the church and gave himself up for her" (5:25). Children are to "obey your parents in the Lord" (6:1). Fathers are to gently bring up their children "in the discipline and instruction of the Lord" (6:4). Slaves are to "obey your earthly masters with fear and trembling, with a sincere heart" (6:5). Masters are to do good to their slaves, knowing they also serve the same Master (6:9).

Paul then reminds the church that we are in the midst of a spiritual battle. "Be strong in the Lord and in the strength of his might," the apostle says. "Put on the whole armor of God, that you may be able to stand against the schemes of the devil" (6:10–11). Living the victorious life God has given us, we are to "stand firm" (6:13), employing God's gifts for the battle: truth, righteousness, evangelism, faith, discernment, "the sword of the Spirit, which is the word of God," and persevering prayer (6:14–20).

God's undeserved heavenly blessings are to be used valiantly here on earth.

50

Philippians 4:4

Rejoice in the Lord always; again I will say, rejoice.

PAUL IS WRITING FROM PRISON TO THE CHURCH HE FOUNDED IN Philippi (Acts 16), thanking its members for their gifts and partnership in his ministry (Phil. 1:1–20; 4:10–20). The theme that winds its way like a golden thread through the epistle is *joy*.

- *Joyful in prayer:* "I thank my God in all my remembrance of you, always in every prayer of mine for you all making my prayer with joy, because of your partnership in the gospel from the first day until now" (1:3–5).
- *Joyful in the gospel:* "What then? Only that in every way, whether in pretense or in truth, Christ is proclaimed, and in that I rejoice" (1:18).
- *Joyful in personal circumstances:* "Yes, and I will rejoice, for I know that through your prayers and the help of the Spirit of Jesus Christ this will turn out for my deliverance" (1:18–19).
- *Joyful in faith:* "Convinced of this, I know that I will remain and continue with you all, for your progress and joy in the faith" (1:25).
- *Joyful in Christian unity:* "Complete my joy by being of the same mind, having the same love, being in full accord and of one mind" (2:2).

- *Joyful in reunions:* "I am the more eager to send [Epaphroditus], therefore, that you may rejoice at seeing him again, and that I may be less anxious. So receive him in the Lord with all joy, and honor such men" (2:28–29).
- *Joyful in the Lord:* "My brothers, rejoice in the Lord" (3:1).
- *Joyful in relationship:* "My brothers, whom I love and long for, my joy and crown, stand firm thus in the Lord, my beloved" (4:1).
- *Joyful in all circumstances: "Rejoice in the Lord always; again I will say, rejoice"* (4:4, emphasis added).
- *Joyful in others' care:* "I rejoiced in the Lord greatly that now at length you have revived your concern for me. You were indeed concerned for me, but you had no opportunity" (4:10).

Paul's joyous thread touches many encouraging truths in Philippians:

- *Our salvation is assured:* "He who began a good work in you will bring it to completion at the day of Jesus Christ" (1:6).
- *God works even in the hard things of life:* "What has happened to me has really served to advance the gospel" (1:12).
- *Death no longer controls us:* "For to me to live is Christ, and to die is gain" (1:21).
- *Christ's humility provides a visible model for our own:* "Have this mind among yourselves, which is yours in Christ Jesus, who, though he was in the form of God, did not count equality with God a thing to be grasped, but emptied himself, by taking the form of a servant, being born in the likeness of men" (2:5–7).
- *God enables us to do his will:* "Work out your own salvation

with fear and trembling, for it is God who works in you, both to will and to work for his good pleasure" (2:12–13).

- *Nothing we have accomplished even remotely compares to the glory of Christ:* "Whatever gain I had, I counted as loss for the sake of Christ. Indeed, I count everything as loss because of the surpassing worth of knowing Christ Jesus my Lord. For his sake I have suffered the loss of all things and count them as rubbish, in order that I may gain Christ" (3:7–8).

- *We are free to live for him:* "Forgetting what lies behind and straining forward to what lies ahead, I press on toward the goal for the prize of the upward call of God in Christ Jesus" (3:13–14).

- *God will give us all that we need in this life:* "My God will supply every need of yours according to his riches in glory in Christ Jesus" (4:19).

Given all this, the command to "rejoice in the Lord always" seems eminently doable.

51

Colossians 1:16

By him all things were created, in heaven and
on earth, visible and invisible, whether thrones
or dominions or rulers or authorities—all things
were created through him and for him.

WHAT DO YOU DO IF YOU ARE STUCK IN PRISON AND A CHURCH YOU
care about is mixing the simple gospel of faith in Christ with a
complicated system that exalts angels and requires fastidious religious practice among its adherents? If you're the apostle Paul, you
write the letter to the Colossians.

Paul did not start the church at Colossae; Epaphras did (1:4–
9). Paul describes Epaphras (apparently not to be confused with
Epaphroditus in Philippians) as our "beloved . . . fellow servant"
and a "faithful minister" of Christ (4:7); "one of you, a servant of
Christ Jesus . . . always struggling on your behalf in his prayers"
(4:12); "he has worked hard for you" (4:13). Epaphras must pray
that the Colossians will be "mature and fully assured in all the
will of God" (4:12) because they aren't.

Their faith is threatened by "philosophy and empty deceit,
according to human tradition, according to the elemental spirits of the world, and not according to Christ" (2:8). An ungodly
legalism is spreading in the fellowship.

"Therefore let no one pass judgment on you in questions of

food and drink, or with regard to a festival or a new moon or a Sabbath," Paul says. "Let no one disqualify you, insisting on asceticism and worship of angels, going on in detail about visions, puffed up without reason by his sensuous mind" (2:16, 18). Paul observes that these teachings have "an appearance of wisdom in promoting self-made religion and asceticism and severity to the body, but they are of no value in stopping the indulgence of the flesh" (2:23).

The answer to any aberrant Christian teaching, quite simply, is a proper understanding of Jesus Christ and what he has done:

> He is the image of the invisible God, the firstborn of all creation. *For by him all things were created, in heaven and on earth, visible and invisible, whether thrones or dominions or rulers or authorities—all things were created through him and for him.* . . . And he is the head of the body, the church. . . . For in him all the fullness of God was pleased to dwell, and through him to reconcile to himself all things, whether on earth or in heaven, making peace by the blood of his cross. (1:15–20, emphasis added)

Jesus Christ is preeminent, the Creator and goal of all things, in both the church and the universe. He has brought God and man together by dying on the cross. Paul reminds the Colossians that Christ's reconciling work includes *them*, "if indeed you continue in the faith, stable and steadfast, not shifting from the hope of the gospel that you heard" (1:23).

"Therefore," Paul writes, "as you received Christ Jesus the Lord, so walk in him, rooted and built up in him and established in the faith, just as you were taught, abounding in thanksgiving" (2:6–7). This walking begins in the mind:

> If then you have been raised with Christ, seek the things that are above, where Christ is, seated at the right hand of God. Set

your minds on things that are above, not on things that are on earth. For you have died, and your life is hidden with Christ in God. When Christ who is your life appears, then you also will appear with him in glory. (3:1–4)

Our focus is to be on Christ in the heavenlies, not on earthly rules and regulations. But this upward focus will naturally lead to practical life changes, by taking out the bad and putting in the good:

- "Put to death therefore what is earthly in you: sexual immorality, impurity, passion, evil desire, and covetousness, which is idolatry" (3:5).
- "Put on then, as God's chosen ones, holy and beloved, compassionate hearts, kindness, humility, meekness, and patience, bearing with one another and, if one has a complaint against another, forgiving each other" (3:12–13).
- "Whatever you do, work heartily, as for the Lord and not for men, knowing that from the Lord you will receive the inheritance as your reward. You are serving the Lord Christ" (3:23–24).

The preeminence of Christ carries immeasurable benefits for his beloved servants, in this life and in the next.

52

1 Thessalonians 5:2

*You yourselves are fully aware that the day of
the Lord will come like a thief in the night.*

WHEN WE READ THE EPISTLES, IT'S A GOOD IDEA TO KEEP A FINGER
or an extra bookmark in Acts, which often provides illuminating
background:

> They came to Thessalonica, where there was a synagogue of
> the Jews. And Paul went in . . . explaining and proving that
> it was necessary for the Christ to suffer and to rise from the
> dead, and saying, "This Jesus, whom I proclaim to you, is the
> Christ." And some of them were persuaded and joined Paul
> and Silas, as did a great many of the devout Greeks and not a
> few of the leading women. But the Jews were jealous, and tak-
> ing some wicked men of the rabble, they formed a mob, set the
> city in an uproar . . . shouting, "These men who have turned
> the world upside down have come here also . . . and they are
> all acting against the decrees of Caesar, saying that there
> is another king, Jesus." And the people and the city authorities
> were disturbed when they heard these things. (Acts 17:1–8)

To save their lives, Paul and Silas had to get out of Dodge in
the dead of night. But Paul agonized over the fate and faith of the

suffering Thessalonian church they had planted, so he sent another helper, Timothy, to check on it (3:6). First Thessalonians is Paul's follow-up letter, dealing with the church's issues and questions that Timothy has shared with him. Paul reminds the believers of his character and their relationship of love (1:5; 2:1–8).

The second coming of Christ looms large in this epistle.[1] These Christians did not know when Christ would return and what difference it ought to make in people's lives now. The second coming has many implications for the believer now:

- *Safety:* "They themselves report concerning us the kind of reception we had among you, and how you turned to God from idols to serve the living and true God, and to wait for his Son from heaven, whom he raised from the dead, Jesus who delivers us from the wrath to come" (1:9–10).
- *Joy:* "What is our hope or joy or crown of boasting before our Lord Jesus at his coming? Is it not you?" (2:19).
- *Purification:* "May the Lord make you increase and abound in love for one another and for all, as we do for you, so that he may establish your hearts blameless in holiness before our God and Father, at the coming of our Lord Jesus with all his saints" (3:12–13).
- *Hope:* "We do not want you to be uninformed, brothers, about those who are asleep, that you may not grieve as others do who have no hope. For since we believe that Jesus died and rose again, even so, through Jesus, God will bring with him those who have fallen asleep. For this we declare to you by a word from the Lord, that we who are alive, who are left until the coming of the Lord, will not precede those who have fallen asleep. For the Lord himself will descend from heaven with a cry of command,

with the voice of an archangel, and with the sound of the trumpet of God. And the dead in Christ will rise first. Then we who are alive, who are left, will be caught up together with them in the clouds to meet the Lord in the air, and so we will always be with the Lord. Therefore encourage one another with these words" (4:13–18).

- *Suddenness:* "Now concerning the times and the seasons, brothers, you have no need to have anything written to you. *For you yourselves are fully aware that the day of the Lord will come like a thief in the night.* While people are saying, 'There is peace and security,' then sudden destruction will come upon them as labor pains come upon a pregnant woman, and they will not escape" (5:1–3, emphasis added).
- *Sanctification:* "Now may the God of peace himself sanctify you completely, and may your whole spirit and soul and body be kept blameless at the coming of our Lord Jesus Christ" (5:23).

Given, as Jesus has said, that the Lord's coming will be like a thief in the night (Matt. 24:43), Christians are to look forward to their salvation (1 Thess. 1:10), be holy (4:1–7), work hard (5:12–15), and experience joy amid their suffering (2:19–20). Living in light of the long-promised "day of the LORD,"[2] which will come suddenly and unexpectedly, is an eminently practical pursuit for Christians in the real world.

53

2 Thessalonians 2:2

*Not to be quickly shaken in mind or alarmed, either by
a spirit or a spoken word, or a letter seeming to be from
us, to the effect that the day of the Lord has come.*

THE OLD TESTAMENT PROPHETS SPOKE OF A COMING "DAY OF THE
LORD" that would signal "the coming time when God will inter-
vene powerfully and decisively in human history to bring about
his promised plan."[1]

> *Woe to you who desire the day of the LORD!*
> *Why would you have the day of the LORD?*
> *It is darkness, and not light. (Amos 5:18)*

> *Wail, for the day of the LORD is near;*
> *as destruction from the Almighty it will come! (Isa. 13:6)*

> *Alas for the day!*
> *For the day of the LORD is near,*
> *and as destruction from the Almighty it comes. (Joel 1:15)*

Although it is sometimes presented as Judgment Day for the
unbelieving nations (Joel 3:14), the day—as the preceding verses
demonstrate—can also bring judgment on unbelieving Israelites.

Old Testament references to the day of the Lord can point to God's use of the pagan nations as rods of his judgment (Isa. 3:18–4:1) or as the day of Israel's future blessing (Isa. 11:11–12).[2] New Testament writers, of course, saw the first and second comings of Christ as aspects of the day of the Lord, with the latter being the ultimate manifestation of God's judgment on sinners and blessing on his people.[3]

It is not surprising, then, that the Thessalonians, already undergoing persecution and with limited access to solid teaching, would be confused about the day of the Lord. Perhaps Paul's earlier statement that the Lord would come like a "thief in the night" had been misunderstood.[4]

Whatever the case, 2 Thessalonians is Paul's attempt to set them straight. The Thessalonians, who were expecting the imminent return of Christ, were unsettled by a false teaching that the day of the Lord—the final "day" that remained for the future—had already happened, and that they had been, to borrow a phrase, left behind.

Judging from Paul's letter, they were "quickly shaken in mind or alarmed, either by a spirit or a spoken word, or a letter seeming to be from us, to the effect that the day of the Lord"—the *final* one—"has come" (2:2). Someone, or some*thing*, perhaps even a counterfeit letter claiming to be from Paul, had told church members, who were experiencing "persecutions [and] afflictions" (1:4), that they had missed out.

So Paul reassures the Thessalonians that Christ has not yet returned by pointing to several key signs about this coming day of the Lord. It will involve the following:

A final rebellion: "That day will not come, unless the rebellion comes first, and the man of lawlessness is revealed, the son of destruction, who opposes and exalts himself against every so-called god or object of worship, so that he takes his seat in the temple of God, proclaiming himself to be God" (2:3–4). An earlier blasphemy was predicted in Daniel 11 and committed during the reign of Antiochus Epiphanes, who profaned the Jewish temple during the second century BC. Jesus indicated that the complete fulfillment of the prophecy was yet in the future.[5]

Ultimate defeat of the lawless one:

The lawless one will be revealed, whom the Lord Jesus will kill with the breath of his mouth and bring to nothing by the appearance of his coming. The coming of the lawless one is by the activity of Satan with all power and false signs and wonders, and with all wicked deception for those who are perishing, because they refused to love the truth and so be saved. Therefore God sends them a strong delusion, so that they may believe what is false, in order that all may be condemned who did not believe the truth but had pleasure in unrighteousness. (2:8–12)

Judgment: God will "grant relief to you who are afflicted as well as to us, when the Lord Jesus is revealed from heaven with his mighty angels in flaming fire, inflicting vengeance on those who do not know God and on those who do not obey the gospel of our Lord Jesus" (1:7–8).

In the meantime, Christians are not to be paralyzed in lethargy or fear. Paul tells the Thessalonians that "walking in idleness" is not God's way (3:6–12). Waiting is always active for believers, as is hope. The Thessalonians have nothing to fear. "The Lord is faithful," Paul says. "He will establish you and guard you against the evil one" (3:3).

54

1 Timothy 3:15

*If I delay, you may know how one ought to behave
in the household of God, which is the church of the
living God, a pillar and buttress of the truth.*

IF YOU ARE TEMPTED TO THINK THAT EPHESIANS SHOWS THAT A
church can have no day-to-day problems,[1] 1 Timothy is there to
set you straight. Written to Timothy, who is both Paul's coworker
and his "true child in the faith" (1:2), this letter instructs a pastor
how to lead his spiritual flock through many challenges. Written
by a man who wants to be in Ephesus personally, the letter—the
first of three Pastoral Epistles—is urgent, brimming with practical instructions for life in the church: "I hope to come to you
soon, but I am writing these things to you so that, *if I delay, you
may know how one ought to behave in the household of God, which is
the church of the living God, a pillar and buttress of the truth*" (3:14–
15, emphasis added).

Church teaching: "As I urged you when I was going to
Macedonia," Paul says, "remain at Ephesus so that you may
charge certain persons not to teach any different doctrine, nor to
devote themselves to myths and endless genealogies, which pro-
mote speculations rather than the stewardship from God that is
by faith" (1:3–4).

These errant teachers have misused the law, a frequent

179

problem in the early churches (Gal. 1:6). They "forbid marriage and require abstinence from foods that God created" (1 Tim. 4:3). Paul says these ideas come from "deceitful spirits and teachings of demons" (4:1). They lead to fractiousness and greed (6:3–10).

Church prayer: Christians are to intercede thankfully "for all people, for kings and for all who are in high positions" (2:1–2). The aim is not only *their* good but "that we may lead a peaceful and quiet life, godly and dignified in every way" (2:2). The reason: "This is good, and it is pleasing in the sight of God our Savior, who desires all people to be saved and to come to the knowledge of the truth" (2:3–4). Prayer is to be done by holy people (2:8).

Church women: Christian women are expected to be modest (2:9), adorned with good works (2:10), and submissive (2:11–12). Paul does not "permit a woman to teach or to exercise authority over a man" because God created Adam first, and Eve was the one who was deceived (2:12–14). Yet just as Eve delivered sons with the Lord's help, leading to the preservation of the human race (Gen. 4:1–2), so the Lord will continue to save women through childbearing (1 Tim. 2:15). The greatest "Son, born of woman," of course, was Jesus, the ultimate Savior (Gal. 4:4).

Church leaders: An overseer (elder) must be "above reproach" in his marriage, family, character, reputation, actions, and teaching (1 Tim. 3:1–5). He must not be new to the faith (3:6). A deacon (Acts 6) is to be truthful, sober, not greedy, and likewise tested (1 Tim. 3:8–10). His family is to match his calling (3:11–13).

Church behavior: All are to be treated with respect and purity (5:1–2). Widows may be helped, but the church is to be discerning (5:3–16). Good elders are "considered worthy of double honor" (5:17). The pastor must "keep these rules without prejudging, doing nothing from partiality" (5:21).

It is a huge job. Aiming to encourage the church to develop a "love that issues from a pure heart and a good conscience and a sincere faith" (1:5), Paul also seeks to encourage Timothy. He tells Timothy "my child" to "wage the good warfare, holding faith and a good conscience" (1:18–19). "If you put these things before the brothers," Paul says, "you will be a good servant of Christ Jesus, being trained in the words of the faith and of the good doctrine that you have followed. . . . [T]rain yourself for godliness. . . . Fight the good fight of the faith. Take hold of the eternal life to which you were called" (4:6–7; 6:12).

Since the church is, according to the key verse, "a pillar and buttress of the truth," Timothy—and every pastor—must hold on to the truth of the gospel. "The saying is trustworthy and deserving of full acceptance," Paul says, "that Christ Jesus came into the world to save sinners, of whom I am the foremost" (1:15). "There is one God," Paul says later, "and there is one mediator between God and men, the man Christ Jesus" (2:5).

Godliness comes not from the law but from the gospel. Truth— right doctrine—somehow mysteriously leads God's people to godly behavior (3:16).

55

2 Timothy 1:8

*Do not be ashamed of the testimony about
our Lord, nor of me his prisoner, but share in
suffering for the gospel by the power of God.*

MARTYRDOM IS STARING THE APOSTLE PAUL IN THE FACE. HIS FINAL
letter chronologically in the New Testament, 2 Timothy is his last
will and testament, given to his ministry assistant "Timothy, my
beloved child" (1:2). Their bond is deeply personal. Paul prays for
Timothy "constantly . . . night and day" (1:3), remembers Timothy's
tears, longs to see him "that I may be filled with joy" (1:4), cherishes
his "sincere faith" (1:5), and asks him to visit in prison (4:9–13).

But because Paul loves Timothy, he is not afraid to exhort him
to stand strong for the gospel: "For this reason I remind you to fan
into flame the gift of God, which is in you through the laying on
of my hands, for God gave us a spirit not of fear but of power and
love and self-control" (1:6–7).

In his loneliness and privation, Paul is concerned that
Timothy might be wavering in his faith. Perhaps Paul's imprisonment has frightened Timothy?

*Do not be ashamed of the testimony about our Lord, nor of me his
prisoner, but share in suffering for the gospel by the power of God,*

who saved us and called us to a holy calling, not because of our works but because of his own purpose and grace.... But I am not ashamed, for I know whom I have believed, and I am convinced that he is able to guard until that Day what has been entrusted to me. (1:8–9, 12, emphasis added)

It is a valid fear. Paul says that "all who are in Asia turned away from me" (1:15). Later, he says, "At my first defense no one came to stand by me, but all deserted me" (4:16). So Paul encourages Timothy to reject any feelings of shame over the gospel and be prepared to suffer for it.

The Christian life is strenuous and full of pain. Rejecting shame means embracing suffering. But Jesus Christ is more than enough for any challenge. "You then, my child, be strengthened by the grace that is in Christ Jesus," Paul says, adding, "share in suffering as a good soldier of Christ Jesus" (2:1, 3). We can do this by keeping our eyes on Jesus (Heb. 12:2). "Remember Jesus Christ," Paul says, "risen from the dead, the offspring of David, as preached in my gospel, for which I am suffering, bound with chains as a criminal" (2:8–9). But Paul is in no way unique in his sufferings. "Indeed," Paul says, "all who desire to live a godly life in Christ Jesus will be persecuted" (3:12).

But Paul eagerly looks past the Christian's temporary suffering to the eternal goal:

> *If we have died with him, we will also live with him;*
> *if we endure, we will also reign with him;*
> *if we deny him, he also will deny us;*
> *if we are faithless, he remains faithful—*
>
> *for he cannot deny himself. (2:11–13)*

So in the meantime Timothy the pastor is to be "a worker who has no need to be ashamed, rightly handling the word of truth" (2:15). He must "avoid irreverent babble" (2:16), "flee youthful passions and pursue righteousness, faith, love, and peace" (2:22), and be a patient and discerning teacher and evangelist (2:23–3:9).

Scripture is to be the pastor's anchor. In contrast to false teachers, Timothy must "continue in what you have learned and have firmly believed . . . the sacred writings, which are able to make you wise for salvation through faith in Christ Jesus" (3:14–15). "All Scripture," Paul continues, "is breathed out by God and profitable for teaching, for reproof, for correction, and for training in righteousness, that the man of God may be complete, equipped for every good work" (3:16–17). It is also to be his spiritual weapon.

Therefore, Paul says, "I charge you in the presence of God and of Christ Jesus, who is to judge the living and the dead, and by his appearing and his kingdom: preach the word; be ready in season and out of season; reprove, rebuke, and exhort, with complete patience and teaching" (4:1–2).

Pastors and all believers who reject shame and embrace suffering for Christ will one day, like Paul, be brought "safely into his heavenly kingdom" (4:18).

56

Titus 3:8

The saying is trustworthy, and I want you to insist on
these things, so that those who have believed in God
may be careful to devote themselves to good works.
These things are excellent and profitable for people.

TITUS IS AN EXCEPTION TO THE GENERAL RULE THAT WE CAN discover the backstory to an epistle by reading Acts. Titus appears nowhere in Luke's account of the expansion of early Christianity. Yet he does show up in some of Paul's other letters, as a "living object lesson . . . that the gospel did not require circumcision of Christian men" and as an emissary "responsible for the collection intended for the poor in Jerusalem," among other duties.[1] Here he is pastoring a church that Paul started in Crete (an action that Acts does not record, meaning the book was probably written after the apostle's first Roman imprisonment and before the second).

The situation in Crete is dire. The church is not in order (1:5). Worse, perhaps, "there are many who are insubordinate, empty talkers and deceivers, especially those of the circumcision party," Paul says. "They . . . are upsetting whole families by teaching for shameful gain what they ought not to teach" (1:10–11). The church's members are "devoting themselves to Jewish myths and the commands of people who turn away from the truth" (1:14).

Using sarcasm to great effect, Paul quotes the sixth-century BC pagan philosopher Epimenides.[2] "One of the Cretans," Paul says, "a prophet of their own, said, 'Cretans are always liars, evil beasts, lazy gluttons.' This testimony is true" (1:12–13).

Therefore, Titus is to use a firm hand to bring order. He must appoint elders (1:5), silence the false teachers (1:11), "teach what accords with sound doctrine" (2:1), "declare these things; exhort and rebuke with all authority" (2:15), "remind them to be submissive to rulers and authorities, to be obedient, to be ready for every good work, to speak evil of no one, to avoid quarreling, to be gentle, and to show perfect courtesy toward all people" (3:1–2).

Titus is thus to focus on both orthodoxy (right doctrine) and orthopraxy (right practice). "The saying is trustworthy," Paul says in the key verse, "and I want you to insist on these things, so that those who have believed in God may be careful to devote themselves to good works. These things are excellent and profitable for people" (3:8). In contrast, the unbelieving "profess to know God, but they deny him by their works. They are detestable, disobedient, unfit for any good work" (1:16).

Paul's instructions for the church are specific. Elders are expected to be "above reproach," being faithful to their wives and raising faithful children (1:6). They must not be arrogant, hotheaded, drunkards, violent, or greedy (1:7). Instead, they must exhibit hospitality, love for the good, self-control, and righteousness (1:8). These character qualities recall the fruit of the Spirit, which Paul lists elsewhere: "love, joy, peace, patience, kindness, goodness, faithfulness, gentleness, [and] self-control" (Gal. 5:22–23).

Church members have their own responsibilities:

- Older men are to be "sober-minded, dignified, self-controlled, sound in faith, in love, and in steadfastness" (Titus 2:2).

- Older women are to be "reverent in behavior, not slanderers or slaves to much wine. They are to teach what is good, and so train the young women" (2:3–4).
- Young women are to "love their husbands and children ... be self-controlled, pure, working at home, kind, and submissive to their own husbands, that the word of God may not be reviled" (2:4–5).
- Younger men are to be "self-controlled" (2:6).
- Pastors (including Titus) are to be models of "good works, and ... show integrity, dignity, and sound speech" in teaching (2:7–8).
- Slaves are to be "submissive to their own masters," "well-pleasing," and "showing all good faith" (2:9–10).

Such expectations are reasonable, given all that God has done for his people, even those of us from Crete:

> We ourselves were once foolish, disobedient, led astray, slaves to various passions and pleasures, passing our days in malice and envy, hated by others and hating one another. But when the goodness and loving kindness of God our Savior appeared, he saved us, not because of works done by us in righteousness, but according to his own mercy, by the washing of regeneration and renewal of the Holy Spirit, whom he poured out on us richly through Jesus Christ our Savior, so that being justified by his grace we might become heirs according to the hope of eternal life. (3:3–7)

Those who *do not believe* cannot *do*. Those who *believe* by God's grace, however, are expected to *do* by that same grace.

57

Philemon 10

*I appeal to you for my child, Onesimus, whose
father I became in my imprisonment.*

PAUL HAS BEEN IMPRISONED, HIS MINISTRY SEEMINGLY NEGATED
by the remorseless Roman Empire. But Paul is not alone. He has
many helpers, including Tychicus, "a beloved brother and faithful
minister and fellow servant in the Lord" (Col. 4:7). Also with the
old apostle in Rome are Aristarchus, "my fellow prisoner"; Mark,
forgiven by Paul and author of the Gospel that bears his name;
Epaphras, who planted the church at Colossae; Luke, who wrote
the third Gospel; and others (4:10–14). Alongside these luminar-
ies is Onesimus, "our faithful and beloved brother" and part of the
Colossian congregation (4:9).

The letter to Philemon provides other details in the life of
Onesimus, whose name means "useful." Our key verse tells us
that this slave became a Christian through Paul's ministry, so
Onesimus is the apostle's spiritual child *and* his spiritual brother.
Formerly strangers in the world, Paul (the great theologian) and
Onesimus (once a pagan slave) have a relationship in Jesus Christ
that transcends human differences. Paul calls Onesimus "my
child" (Phil. 10), "useful" (11), "my very heart" (12), and a vital
help to Paul in his imprisonment (13).

Yet Onesimus has a dark chapter in his past. Though named

"useful," he was "useless" as a slave to Philemon (11). He apparently stole from his master (18) before fleeing from Colossae, in modern-day Turkey, and eventually meeting Paul in Rome (15), some twelve hundred miles to the west.

First-century slavery, though certainly far from ideal, is not to be confused with the race-based monstrosity later imposed on blacks in the West. "In the world of the New Testament, slavery was not race-specific, as we think of slavery in our own American experience," Mark Dever writes. "Nor were slaves limited to certain types of jobs. In most Hellenic cities of Paul's day, the majority of the working population [was] probably considered slaves, or what might be called indentured servants."[1]

Some slaves signed up voluntarily and were treated well, even sometimes as members of the family, but the institution was no paradise (Eph. 6:5–9). Always looming in the background was the threat of force. Indeed, a runaway slave, as Onesimus was, faced a possible death sentence if caught.

Yes, Philemon is Paul's "beloved fellow worker" (Phil. 1) and someone who loves Christ and his church (2, 5). But Philemon is also a slave owner. He owns Onesimus, and he holds all the cards. The epistle, presumably accompanied by the converted Onesimus himself, is Paul's attempt to get his friend and fellow minister to "receive [Onesimus] as you would receive me" (17). To win Philemon's assent, Paul does not simply assert his spiritual authority as an apostle (9). Instead, he seeks to win the slave owner's heart (14).

Paul informs Philemon about how Onesimus has become dear to him in his imprisonment (10, 12). Onesimus, formerly "useless" to Philemon (11), has become precious in his service to the apostle, even serving on behalf of Philemon (13)! A pilfering runaway slave's life has been transformed by the gospel.

Then Paul tells Philemon that this fact ought to impact how

the two men relate to each other in the future: "This perhaps is why he was parted from you for a while, that you might have him back forever, no longer as a bondservant but more than a bond-servant, as a beloved brother—especially to me, but how much more to you, both in the flesh and in the Lord" (15–16).

Philemon and Onesimus are not only equals; they are broth-ers—and beloved ones at that. Given this truth, though Paul doesn't say so explicitly, slavery is no longer an option. As the church gradually came to understand and apply the gospel (and the book of Philemon) in the succeeding centuries, it is no wonder that, for most, the old institution was no longer thinkable.

Paul clinches his appeal to Philemon with practical matters. If Onesimus has stolen anything, Paul says he will pay the debt (18)—adding ironically, "to say nothing of your owing me even your own self" (19).

Having already commended Philemon in his short appeal for having "refreshed" fellow Christians (7), Paul now commands him: "Refresh my heart in Christ" (20). It is a command that can have only one response: "Confident of your obedience, I write to you, knowing that you will do even more than I say" (21). The relationship of Philemon and Onesimus, once a matter of power and obligation, will henceforth be characterized by dignity and love, one that Paul, looking ahead to his eventual release, will wit-ness firsthand (22).

58

Hebrews 4:14

*Since then we have a great high priest who
has passed through the heavens, Jesus, the Son
of God, let us hold fast our confession.*

NO ONE KNOWS THE AUTHOR OF HEBREWS. "WHO ACTUALLY WROTE
the epistle," Eusebius stated in his *Ecclesiastical History*, "only God
knows."[1] Yet the reason for the letter is crystal clear. The recipients are in danger of giving up their faith:

> We must pay much closer attention to what we have heard, lest
> we drift away from it. . . . [H]ow shall we escape if we neglect
> such a great salvation? (2:1, 3)

> Take care, brothers, lest there be in any of you an evil,
> unbelieving heart, leading you to fall away from the living
> God. But exhort one another every day . . . that none of you
> may be hardened by the deceitfulness of sin. (3:12–13)

Suffering for their faith (12:3), they are being tempted to give
up or soft-pedal their allegiance to Christ by returning to Judaism.
The author encourages them to stand firm. Jesus, he says, is greater
than all who have come before because only *he* is God's Son:

Long ago, at many times and in many ways, God spoke to our fathers by the prophets, but in these last days he has spoken to us by his Son, whom he appointed the heir of all things, through whom also he created the world. He is the radiance of the glory of God and the exact imprint of his nature, and he upholds the universe by the word of his power. (1:1–3)

As such, Jesus is superior to God's angels (1:4–2:8), to God's faithful servant, Moses (3:1–6), and to God's Levitical priesthood (4:14–10:18). As a result, we must cling to *him* for salvation, which the author calls God's rest, a rest that the unbelieving Israelites failed to enter after the Exodus: "Let us therefore strive to enter that rest, so that no one may fall by the same sort of disobedience. . . . *Since then we have a great high priest who has passed through the heavens, Jesus, the Son of God, let us hold fast our confession*" (4:11, 14, emphasis added).

Yet the author reminds us that Jesus is not only better; he is kinder. "For we do not have a high priest who is unable to sympathize with our weaknesses, but one who in every respect has been tempted as we are, yet without sin," he writes. "Let us then with confidence draw near to the throne of grace, that we may receive mercy and find grace to help in time of need" (4:15–16).

In chapter 11, the author points out that we live this kind of life by faith, which is "the assurance of things hoped for, the conviction of things not seen" (11:1). Such faith is not only good; it is indispensable for life with God because "without faith it is impossible to please him" (11:6). And while faith believes without seeing, it still has many real-world examples to emulate.

"By faith" Noah built the ark (11:7); Abraham and Sarah were the progenitors of God's people (11:8–19); Isaac blessed Jacob and Esau (11:20); Jacob worshipfully blessed Joseph's sons (11:21); Joseph cast his lot with God's people (11:22); Moses chose "rather to be mistreated with the people of God than to enjoy the fleeting pleasures of sin" (11:25); the people crossed the Red Sea (11:29); the walls of Jericho fell down (11:30); and Rahab welcomed the spies (11:31).

And there were others "who through faith conquered kingdoms, enforced justice, obtained promises, stopped the mouths of lions, quenched the power of fire," and more (11:32–35). Some of them suffered grievously by that same faith (11:35–38). And they are more than examples; our fate and faith are bound up with theirs (11:39–40).

Not surprisingly, the premier example of persevering faith is Jesus, "who for the joy that was set before him endured the cross . . . and is seated at the right hand of the throne of God" (12:2). The author then instructs us: "Consider him who endured from sinners such hostility against himself, so that you may not grow weary or fainthearted" (12:3). We also must remember that God allows us to suffer because we are his children who need discipline (12:7–11).

Closing the argument, the author reiterates that the covenant brought by Jesus the Son is superior to the Old Testament covenant (12:22–24) and adds, "Therefore let us be grateful for receiving a kingdom that cannot be shaken, and thus let us offer to God acceptable worship, with reverence and awe, for our God is a consuming fire" (12:28–29).

Our response to the Son's gracious offer of forgiveness is of monumental importance.

59

James 1:22

Be doers of the word, and not hearers
only, deceiving yourselves.

JAMES, ONE OF SEVERAL MEN IN THE NEW TESTAMENT SO NAMED,[1] was a person of faith and action. A brother of Jesus (Matt. 13:55) and initially a skeptic (John 7:5), he eventually became an active believer in the risen Lord (1 Cor. 15:7). James was a leader in the Jerusalem church (Acts 12; 15; 21). He was "so often found kneeling in prayer for the people that his knees grew hard like a camel's."[2] In AD 62, James was "thrown from the parapet of the temple, stoned, and finally killed by a blow from a fuller's club."[3] After James came to faith and until his martyrdom, he was all in.

In the book that bears his name, James exhibits that same commitment. Aware of the suffering that often accompanies faith in the Messiah, he writes to Jewish believers (1:1) who are facing "trials of various kinds" (1:2), encouraging them to remain "steadfast" so that they will "receive the crown of life, which God has promised to those who love him" (1:12). Patience for such a life of faith is mandatory (5:7–11).

James says that faith in Christ must produce changed attitudes and actions. There are many *attitudes* to avoid:

- *Anger:* Followers of Christ are to control their tempers, "for the anger of man does not produce the righteousness of God" (1:20). We must "receive with meekness the implanted word, which is able to save your souls" (1:21).
- *Partiality:* We shouldn't favor the rich over the poor in our assemblies (2:1–11).
- *Judgmentalism:* Those who have shown no mercy cannot expect to receive it (2:12–13; Matt. 5:7).
- *Jealousy:* Ambition for self must be replaced by "wisdom from above," which is "first pure, then peaceable, gentle, open to reason, full of mercy and good fruits, impartial and sincere" (3:17).
- *Selfish pride:* Believers must avoid worldliness (4:1–12) and arrogance (4:13–16).
- *Coveting:* The stingy rich are advised to "weep and howl for the miseries that are coming upon you" (5:1).

However, right attitudes are not enough. They must lead to right *actions*. "Be doers of the word," James says in the key verse, "and not hearers only, deceiving yourselves" (1:22). It is a familiar refrain:

What good is it, my brothers, if someone says he has faith but does not have works? Can that faith save him? If a brother or sister is poorly clothed and lacking in daily food, and one of you says to them, "Go in peace, be warmed and filled," without giving them the things needed for the body, what good is that? So also faith by itself, if it does not have works, is dead. (2:14–17)

Showing the insufficiency of a faith bereft of works, James (much like Heb. 11) illustrates how true faith is active, as in the lives of Abraham and Rahab (2:18–25). A lack of faithful activity indicates a lack of life: "For as the body apart from the spirit is dead, so also faith apart from works is dead" (2:26).

There are many right actions enjoined for the Christian.

- *Mercy ministries:* "Religion that is pure and undefiled before God, the Father, is this: to visit orphans and widows in their affliction, and to keep oneself unstained from the world" (1:27).
- *Control of our speech:* "For every kind of beast and bird, of reptile and sea creature, can be tamed and has been tamed by mankind, but no human being can tame the tongue. It is a restless evil, full of deadly poison. With it we bless our Lord and Father, and with it we curse people who are made in the likeness of God. From the same mouth come blessing and cursing. My brothers, these things ought not to be so" (3:7–10).
- *Holiness:* "Submit yourselves therefore to God. Resist the devil, and he will flee from you. Draw near to God, and he will draw near to you. Cleanse your hands, you sinners, and purify your hearts, you double-minded. Be wretched and mourn and weep. Let your laughter be turned to mourning and your joy to gloom. Humble yourselves before the Lord, and he will exalt you" (4:7–10).
- *Prayer in all the exigencies of life:* "The prayer of a righteous person has great power as it is working" (5:16).

In all these actions that flow from our faith, we will be clear-eyed "doers of the word."

60

1 Peter 4:13

Rejoice insofar as you share Christ's sufferings, that you
may also rejoice and be glad when his glory is revealed.

PETER'S FIRST EPISTLE, TO THE "ELECT EXILES OF THE DISPERSION
in Pontus, Galatia, Cappadocia, Asia, and Bithynia" (1:1), is the
old apostle's call for Christians to embrace suffering as the path
to future glory. This is no religious cliché for Peter, who rejected
the cross twice (Matt. 16:21–23; 26:69–75) before embracing his
eventual death on a Roman cross (John 21:18–19). Peter, "a witness of the sufferings of Christ, as well as a partaker in the glory
that is going to be revealed" (1 Peter 5:1), urges believers to take
the same heavenly perspective amid their earthly trials. That's
because suffering and glory are inextricably bound. He says,

> Beloved, do not be surprised at the fiery trial when it comes
> upon you to test you, as though something strange were hap-
> pening to you. *But rejoice insofar as you share Christ's sufferings,*
> *that you may also rejoice and be glad when his glory is revealed.*
> If you are insulted for the name of Christ, you are blessed,
> because the Spirit of glory and of God rests upon you. (4:12–
> 14, emphasis added)

Suffering is not simply a necessary evil to be endured but a sign pointing to a sure future reward. Just as we will rejoice *then*, we ought to rejoice *now*. This perspective on the two realities calls to mind the Lord's words in the Sermon on the Mount: "Blessed are you when others revile you and persecute you and utter all kinds of evil against you falsely on my account. Rejoice and be glad, for your reward is great in heaven, for so they persecuted the prophets who were before you" (Matt. 5:11–12).

Such heavenly mindedness leads to earthly rejoicing. We possess "a living hope through the resurrection of Jesus Christ from the dead . . . an inheritance that is imperishable, undefiled, and unfading, kept in heaven for you . . . a salvation ready to be revealed in the last time" (1 Peter 1:3–5). Our present bitter circumstances make our promised future glory all the sweeter:

> In this you rejoice, though now for a little while, if necessary, you have been grieved by various trials, so that the tested genuineness of your faith—more precious than gold that perishes though it is tested by fire—may be found to result in praise and glory and honor at the revelation of Jesus Christ. Though you have not seen him, you love him. Though you do not now see him, you believe in him and rejoice with joy that is inexpressible and filled with glory, obtaining the outcome of your faith, the salvation of your souls. (1:6–9)

Such future hope also leads to present faithfulness. Peter calls on believers to be holy (1:14–21; 2:11–12; 4:1–11); loving (1:22–23); truthful (2:1); longing for God's Word (2:2–3); submissive "to every human institution" (2:13–25); committed to their marriages (3:1–7); patient in suffering (3:8–22; 4:12–19; 5:8–9); eager as church leaders (5:1–5); and humble. "Clothe yourselves, all of you, with humility toward one another, for 'God opposes the proud but gives grace to the humble,'" Peter commands. "Humble yourselves, therefore, under the mighty hand of God so that at the proper time he may exalt you, casting all your anxieties on him, because he cares for you" (5:5–7).

Such humility is possible not because we have self-confidence but because we have *God*-confidence: "After you have suffered a little while, the God of all grace, who has called you to his eternal glory in Christ, will himself restore, confirm, strengthen, and establish you" (5:10).

God's grace, which gives future hope in the midst of present suffering, suffuses the epistle. Because of our "sprinkling with [Christ's] blood," believers receive God's "grace and peace . . . multiplied" (1:2), even in the sometimes grim here and now. This salvation was predicted by the prophets, longed for by angels, and heard by believers (1:10–12). We are "a royal priesthood . . . God's people" (2:9–10).

"Therefore," Peter says, "preparing your minds for action, and being sober-minded, set your hope fully on the grace that will be brought to you at the revelation of Jesus Christ" (1:13).

61

2 Peter 3:2

*You should remember the predictions of the
holy prophets and the commandment of the
Lord and Savior through your apostles.*

WRITING FROM A ROMAN PRISON, PETER IS NEAR THE END OF HIS
earthly life and ministry, so he is leaving Christians—"those who
have obtained a faith of equal standing with ours by the righteousness of our God and Savior Jesus Christ" (1:1)—his final
instructions. "I think it is right," he says, "as long as I am in this
body, to stir you up by way of reminder, since I know that the putting off of my body will be soon, as our Lord Jesus Christ made
clear to me" (1:13–14).[1]

The task is urgent for Peter, who later says, "This is now the
second letter that I am writing to you, beloved. In both of them I
am stirring up your sincere mind by way of reminder," adding his
purpose for the letter, *"that you should remember the predictions
of the holy prophets and the commandment of the Lord and Savior
through your apostles"* (3:1–2, emphasis added).

The predictions of the holy prophets. Although prophecies come
from the mouths (and pens) of prophets, Peter is careful to point to
their divine source: "No prophecy of Scripture comes from someone's own interpretation. For no prophecy was ever produced by

the will of man, but men spoke from God as they were carried along by the Holy Spirit" (1:20–21).

The prophecies Peter has in mind point to the Second Coming. They will not be popular, the apostle warns: "Scoffers will come in the last days. . . . They will say, 'Where is the promise of his coming? For ever since the fathers fell asleep, all things are continuing as they were from the beginning of creation'" (3:3–4).

Peter points out that the Flood refutes this sinful assumption (3:5–6) and foreshadows an even greater judgment to come (3:7–9). "The day of the Lord will come like a thief," he warns, "and then the heavens will pass away with a roar, and the heavenly bodies will be burned up and dissolved, and the earth and the works that are done on it will be exposed" (3:10). Such prophecies have a sanctifying purpose in believers' lives: "Since all these things are thus to be dissolved, what sort of people ought you to be in lives of holiness and godliness!" (3:11).

The commandment of the Lord. Yet Christ's holy and godly people get this way not by their efforts but by "his divine power [which] has granted to us all things that pertain to life and godliness, . . . [making us] partakers of the divine nature" (1:3–4).

Our role is not passive, however. We are to "make every effort to supplement [our] faith with virtue, and virtue with knowledge, and knowledge with self-control, and self-control with steadfastness, and steadfastness with godliness, and godliness with brotherly affection, and brotherly affection with love" (1:5–7).

We are called to lives of God-empowered effort. "Therefore, brothers," Peter says, "be all the more diligent to confirm your calling and election, for if you practice these qualities you will never fall" (1:10).

Through your apostles. Though Peter is gentle, he is firm. We are to follow the apostles' teaching and no one else's. "We did not follow cleverly devised myths when we made known to you the power and coming of our Lord Jesus Christ," he asserts, "but we were eyewitnesses of his majesty" (1:16). The apostles offer something more sure than a heavenly voice: "the prophetic word . . . to which you will do well to pay attention" (1:19).

This is in contrast to false prophets and teachers, "who will secretly bring in destructive heresies, even denying the Master who bought them, bringing upon themselves swift destruction" (2:1). Peter describes their bitter fruit and fearsome judgment in detail (2:2–22). "These are waterless springs and mists driven by a storm," Peter says (2:17). His grim assessment brings to mind this description of the wicked: they are "like chaff that the wind drives away" (Ps. 1:4).

In contrast, the apostle says that believers are to follow the Lord's call to "be diligent to be found by [God] without spot or blemish, and at peace" (2 Peter 3:14). As we await the Lord's return, we are to "grow in the grace and knowledge of our Lord and Savior Jesus Christ" (3:18).

62

1 John 1:3

That which we have seen and heard we proclaim
also to you, so that you too may have fellowship
with us; and indeed our fellowship is with the
Father and with his Son Jesus Christ.

FOR THE APOSTLE JOHN, THE CHRISTIAN'S HOPE BEGINS WITH THE
incarnation, to which he is an eyewitness:[1]

> That which was from the beginning, which we have heard, which
> we have seen with our eyes, which we looked upon and have
> touched with our hands, concerning the word of life—the
> life was made manifest, and we have seen it, and testify to it
> and proclaim to you the eternal life, which was with the Father
> and was made manifest to us. (1:1–2)

John sees his calling as proclaiming Jesus, who was "from the
beginning" but who nevertheless was accessible to human beings
during his earthly life and ministry. Then in the next verse the
apostle tells why he is proclaiming the incarnated Lord: *"so that
you too may have fellowship with us; and indeed our fellowship is with
the Father and with his Son Jesus Christ"* (1:3, emphasis added).

John seeks to share the fellowship ("the common experience/
sharing of something with someone else"[2]) he already enjoys

with the Father and the Son with other believers. His goal: "We are writing these things so that our joy may be complete" (1:4). Fellowship is based on Jesus the God-man and has both horizontal and vertical elements, bringing joy to all.

That which we have seen and heard. John is careful to describe who Jesus is and what he has done: "the life . . . made manifest . . . the eternal life . . . with the Father" (1:2); the "Son" (1:3, 7; 4:15; 5:10–13); provides cleansing blood (1:7; 5:6); "the righteous" (2:1); "the propitiation for our sins . . . also for the sins of the whole world" (2:2; 4:10); giver of commandments (2:3–6); the Christ (2:22; 5:1); "destroy[s] the works of the devil" (3:8); "has come in the flesh" (4:2); "the Savior of the world" (4:14); "has given us understanding, so that we may know him who is true. . . . [T]he true God and eternal life" (5:20).

So that you too may have fellowship with us. Believer-to-believer fellowship, based on Christ, occurs frequently in 1 John. It means we will "walk in the light, as he is in the light" (1:7); love our Christian brothers and sisters (2:7–11; 3:11–18; 5:1–2); test the spirits for their fidelity to Christ (4:1–6); intercede for a sinning brother (5:16–17); and avoid idols (5:21). "Whoever loves his brother abides in the light, and in him there is no cause for stumbling," John says. "But whoever hates his brother is in the darkness and walks in the darkness, and does not know where he is going, because the darkness has blinded his eyes" (2:10–11).

Our fellowship is with the Father and with his Son. John discusses vertical fellowship—that which occurs between the believer and the triune God (including the Spirit, 3:24; 4:13)—frequently. It involves walking in the light (1:6–10); obeying his commands (2:1–6); receiving God's forgiveness (2:7–14); refusing to love the sinful world (2:15–17); rejecting falsehood and abiding in God's truth (2:18–27); practicing righteousness and avoiding sin (2:28–3:9; 5:18); loving one's brother (3:10; 4:7–12, 19–21;

5:2–4); experiencing confidence before God (3:19–24; 4:17–18; 5:13–15, 19); and believing and confessing that Jesus is the Son of God (4:13–16; 5:1, 5–12, 20).

Such signs of our vertical fellowship with God naturally affect our horizontal fellowship with other Christians. "Everyone who believes that Jesus is the Christ has been born of God," John writes, "and everyone who loves the Father loves whoever has been born of him" (5:1).

Christian fellowship, founded on Christ, produces joy that we experience today and will enjoy throughout eternity. "Beloved," John writes, "we are God's children now, and what we will be has not yet appeared; but we know that when he appears we shall be like him, because we shall see him as he is. And everyone who thus hopes in him purifies himself as he is pure" (3:2–3).

63

2 John 6

This is love, that we walk according to his commandments;
this is the commandment, just as you have heard
from the beginning, so that you should walk in it.

WRITING FROM EPHESUS SOMETIME NEAR THE END OF THE FIRST
century, John "the elder" sends a letter "to the elect lady and her
children" (1). The last surviving apostle, John is indeed an elder,
both spiritually and physically. Many scholars believe the recipient is a church,[1] which would track with John's understanding
stated elsewhere that believers constitute the bride of Christ, who
is our Bridegroom (John 3:29; Rev. 21:9). Perhaps John is using
coded language during a time of persecution, as many Christians
around the world are forced to do today.

In a Bible book that could fit onto the back of an envelope,
right from the start the author links love and light, faith and obedience, addressing his remarks to those "whom I love in truth" (1).
There is no genuine love without truth. Driving home the point,
John adds that this church is loved by "all who know the truth,
because of the truth that abides in us and will be with us forever"
(1–2). Then he points out the reward of our faithful love: "Grace,
mercy, and peace will be with us, from God the Father and from
Jesus Christ the Father's Son, in truth and love" (3).

This dual emphasis on love and truth in the opening verses

calls to mind earlier statements John heard direct from the lips of Jesus:

- "I am the way, and the truth, and the life" (John 14:6). He is not just one source of truth—he is "*the* truth." He is also "*the* way" and "*the* life." Truth is inseparable from our lives as believers.
- "If you love me, you will keep my commandments" (John 14:15). Just as Old Testament saints demonstrated their love for God by how they obeyed him, so do New Testament saints.

John says he "rejoiced greatly to find some of your children walking in the truth" (2 John 4). The walk of a Christian is important to the apostle, who has already commanded us to "walk in the light, as he is in the light" (1 John 1:7). We are to live in the light of, and according to, God's truth. As the key verse says, "This is love, that we walk according to his commandments; this is the commandment, just as you have heard from the beginning, so that you should walk in it" (2 John 6).

The "commandment" to which John refers may be this one from the Lord's Upper Room Discourse: "A new commandment I give to you, that you love one another: just as I have loved you, you also are to love one another" (John 13:34). Yes, commandment and love go together. In fact, we are commanded *to* love.

If love for the truth characterizes the Christian, however, then so does its flip side: hatred for falsehood. That is because lies, especially those that deny Christ and his teaching, come from the devil, "the father of lies" (John 8:44). Those who promulgate these deceptions wage war against Christ and his church, threatening men's souls and our heavenly rewards. We are to avoid such people:

Many deceivers have gone out into the world, those who do not confess the coming of Jesus Christ in the flesh. Such a one is the deceiver and the antichrist. Watch yourselves, so that you may not lose what we have worked for, but may win a full reward. Everyone who goes on ahead and does not abide in the teaching of Christ, does not have God. Whoever abides in the teaching has both the Father and the Son. If anyone comes to you and does not bring this teaching, do not receive him into your house or give him any greeting, for whoever greets him takes part in his wicked works. (2 John 7–11)

John closes his letter by sharing his desire for a face-to-face meeting, "so that our joy may be complete" (12). John's love for the church, based on the truth that is in Christ, is a model for our own.

64

3 John 8

*We ought to support people like these, that
we may be fellow workers for the truth.*

THERE ARE SEVERAL MEN NAMED GAIUS IN THE NEW TESTAMENT,
including the recipient of 3 John.[1] In a Bible book shorter than
some grocery lists, we know very little about *this* Gaius. According
to the epistle, Gaius

- is spiritually healthy (2);
- is "walking in the truth"[2] (3);
- is a spiritual child of John (4);
- has supported Christian missionaries (5);
- is a man of love (6); and
- is loved by John and other believers (13–15).

Indeed, John addresses Gaius as "Beloved" three times:

- "Beloved, I pray that all may go well with you and that you
  may be in good health, as it goes well with your soul" (2).
- "Beloved, it is a faithful thing you do in all your efforts
  for these brothers, strangers as they are" (5).
- "Beloved, do not imitate evil but imitate good" (11).

John the apostle loves to tell fellow believers that they are "beloved" (1 John 3:2). Gaius apparently is no one special in the world's economy, though he certainly is in God's. He is *beloved*. In these three verses, beloved Gaius is the object of John's prayer, John's commendation, and John's command.

Gaius has already done much that is worthy of imitation. He has supported some unnamed missionaries—those sent out in the name of Christ. In this letter, John calls on Gaius to continue his "faithful" work. Any kind of material support of Christian work is an act of faith, of course. It is an investment not in the kingdom of this world but in what ultimately the world will become under Jesus Christ's rule (Rev. 11:15). John says,

> Beloved, it is a faithful thing you do in all your efforts for these brothers, strangers as they are, who testified to your love before the church. You will do well to send them on their journey in a manner worthy of God. For they have gone out for the sake of the name, accepting nothing from the Gentiles. *Therefore we ought to support people like these, that we may be fellow workers for the truth.* (3 John 5–8, emphasis added)

This act of sacrifice—even for strangers—takes faith, love, and effort, but it receives the Lord's commendation. Not only this, but we become "fellow workers for the truth" when we help Christian workers. Not every Christian may be called or gifted to go as a missionary (someone sent as an emissary of Christ), but all are called to *support* missionaries. When we respond to the Lord's call to share our resources faithfully—and this requires perseverance to keep on going—we are credited in the Lord's account books with working alongside them in gospel ministry.

Though aware of his apostolic authority in dealing with unfaithful men (9–10), John does not separate himself from ordinary men such as Gaius (and Demetrius, another faithful worker [12]). In God's kingdom, they are all "friends" (13–15). Such a designation calls to mind Jesus' words to the disciples in the Upper Room, as recorded by John:

> Greater love has no one than this, that someone lay down his life for his friends. You are my friends if you do what I command you. No longer do I call you servants, for the servant does not know what his master is doing; but I have called you friends, for all that I have heard from my Father I have made known to you. You did not choose me, but I chose you and appointed you that you should go and bear fruit and that your fruit should abide, so that whatever you ask the Father in my name, he may give it to you. (John 15:13–16)

Friendship speaks of intimacy and belonging. If the Lord Jesus can deign to consider *us* as his friends, is there any doubt that believers can consider *one another* as friends? And as friends of God and one another, we are called, as Gaius was, not to work the harvest field alone but to bear fruit *together*.

65

Jude 3

*Beloved, although I was very eager to write to you
about our common salvation, I found it necessary
to write appealing to you to contend for the faith
that was once for all delivered to the saints.*

JUDE, A LESSER-KNOWN BROTHER OF THE LORD JESUS,¹ CALLS
himself merely "a servant of Jesus Christ and brother of James" (1).
In this brief but urgent letter, the author explains that he has shelved
his plan to write an encouraging epistle about doctrine. Instead, as
the key verse reveals, the letter has become a call to battle: "Beloved,
although I was very eager to write to you about our common salvation, I found it necessary to write appealing to you to contend for
the faith that was once for all delivered to the saints" (3).

Jude's change of plans has occurred because "certain people have
crept in unnoticed" (4)—except by *God*, who "long ago [desig-
nated]" them for "this condemnation" (4). They are "ungodly
people, who pervert the grace of our God into sensuality and deny
our only Master and Lord, Jesus Christ" (4). Their lives are characterized by sinful actions and damnable heresy, which often go
together.

The people to whom Jude writes "once fully knew" that "Jesus,
who saved a people out of the land of Egypt, afterward destroyed
those who did not believe" (5).² The implication is that these

believers are wavering on account of the ungodly false teachers and face possible judgment. Jude warns his readers that we can see a preview of what God's judgment of "eternal fire" looks like in his destruction of Sodom and Gomorrah—a judgment that awaits even apostate angels (6–7).

Next, Jude returns to the ungodly character and actions of "these people" (8). They rely on their own dreams (rather than "the faith that was once for all delivered to the saints" [3]). In other words, they have no authority for their teaching other than themselves (8). They "defile the flesh" (8), implying sexual immorality. They even blaspheme angels (8) as well as "all that they do not understand, and they are destroyed by all that they, like unreasoning animals, understand instinctively" (10). For these sinners, their ignorance of sacred things and their knowledge of earthly things lead to ruin.

"Woe to them!" Jude pronounces, drawing on rich Old Testament and Jewish literature (11, 14–15). The ungodly teachers are like Cain, a jealous murderer; Balaam, a greedy false prophet; and Korah, who rebelled against God-ordained authority (11). They are dangerous like "hidden reefs" (12); they behave as selfish "shepherds feeding themselves" rather than providing for the sheep (12).

Then Jude's imagery becomes truly terrifying. They are "waterless clouds, swept along by winds; fruitless trees in late autumn, twice dead, uprooted; wild waves of the sea, casting up the foam of their own shame; wandering stars, for whom the gloom of utter darkness has been reserved forever" (12–13).

Quoting Enoch (14–15), Jude says the judgment of God and his angels is coming "to convict all the ungodly of all their deeds of ungodliness that they have committed in such an ungodly way, and of all the harsh things that ungodly sinners have spoken against him" (15–16). As Jesus said elsewhere, we will be judged based on our deeds[3] and our words[4] (16). The ultimate sin of the lost is that they are ungodly.

Jude then encourages those he has already called "beloved in God the Father and kept for Jesus Christ" (1) to stand fast (17–23). They must

- remember that the apostles predicted these false teachers (17–19);
- keep themselves in the love of God by building themselves up in the "most holy faith," "praying in the Holy Spirit," and "waiting for the mercy of our Lord Jesus Christ that leads to eternal life" (20–21); and
- have mercy on those struggling with doubt; those in danger of hell (presumably through unbelief); and those who are enmeshed in sin (22–23).

Closing his spiritual call to arms, Jude reassures his beloved readers with this beautiful doxology: "Now to him who is able to keep you from stumbling and to present you blameless before the presence of his glory with great joy, to the only God, our Savior, through Jesus Christ our Lord, be glory, majesty, dominion, and authority, before all time and now and forever. Amen" (24–25).

Though they face a tremendous, high-stakes struggle, these believers can move forward with confidence because of *God's* love and faithfulness.

66

Revelation 1:19

Write therefore the things that you have seen, those
that are and those that are to take place after this.

REVELATION IS A BOOK ABOUT WHAT GOD WILL DO IN THE FUTURE.
Yet, as most works of prophecy are, it is also about living for the
Lord in the present.[1]

The opening (1:1–8) describes the book's title ("the revelation of Jesus Christ"), mode of transmission ("by sending his
angel"), author ("to his servant John, who bore witness . . . to all
that he saw"), intended effect ("Blessed is the one who reads . . .
and blessed are those who hear"), time frame ("the time is near"),
recipients ("seven churches . . . in Asia"), lead character ("him
who is and who was and who is to come . . . the faithful witness . . .
the firstborn of the dead . . . the ruler of kings on the earth . . . who
loves us and has freed us from our sins by his blood"), and ending
("he is coming with the clouds, and every eye will see him").

Though the apocalyptic symbols and events in Revelation can
be difficult and complex, the book's outline[2] is straightforward.
"Write therefore the things that you have seen," John is instructed
in the key verse, "those that are and those that are to take place
after this" (1:19).

Those that are:

1:9–20: On Patmos, John encounters the risen Lord. "The hairs of his head were white," the apostle reports. "His eyes were like a flame of fire, his feet were like burnished bronze, refined in a furnace, and his voice was like the roar of many waters" (1:14–15).

2:1–3:22: Christ dictates letters to the seven churches of Asia Minor—Ephesus (2:1–7), Smyrna (2:8–11), Pergamum (2:12–17), Thyatira (2:18–29), Sardis (3:1–6), Philadelphia (3:7–13), and Laodicea (3:14–22). Each letter contains some combination of a description of the Lord, a commendation, a criticism, a way out, a warning, and a promise.[3]

Each letter encourages or warns its hearers to remain faithful to Christ. Only two churches, Smyrna and Philadelphia, receive no rebuke, as they faithfully endure persecution. Only one, the worldly Laodicea, earns no commendation. All are told repeatedly to listen: "He who has an ear, let him hear what the Spirit says to the churches." We must persevere to receive our Lord's commendation and rewards.

Those that are to take place:

4:1–22:5: The second (and main) division of Revelation describes "what must take place after this" (4:1). After experiencing a glorious vision of heaven (4), John sees the worthy Lamb (Jesus)[4] take a scroll with seven seals (5). These are opened (6:1–8:5), as God's judgment on his enemies unfolds. Then seven trumpets sound in response to the prayers of the saints (8:6–11:18).[5] More destruction ensues, with locusts, plagues, and fire.

Chapter 12 seems to present the perennial conflict between the dragon and the child of a woman—that is, between Satan and the Lord Jesus Christ, who prevailed in his death and resurrection. "Then the dragon became furious with the woman," we are told, "and went off to make war on the rest of her offspring, on those who keep the commandments of God and hold to the testimony of Jesus" (12:17). Christians can expect tribulation in this world—ultimately followed by their participation in Christ's victory.

After describing the conflict between the beasts (stand-ins for Satan) and the Lamb (13–14), John presents his final series of seven—the seven bowls of God's wrath (15–16). Then Babylon falls (17:1–19:10); the dragon and his emissaries are defeated (19:11–20:10); and the final judgment is announced (20:11–15).

In fulfillment of prophecy in both Old and New Testaments, the cosmos is remade (21:9–22:5).[6] We glimpse a new heaven and earth, a perfected Jerusalem, and the end of all suffering, as the Lord of the universe makes his everlasting abode with his now sinless and joyful people. It is a consummation that fulfills and even surpasses the relationship we enjoyed with our Creator in the garden—a relationship, now as always, received by faith: "They will see his face, and his name will be on their foreheads. And night will be no more. They will need no light of lamp or sun, for the Lord God will be their light, and they will reign forever and ever" (22:4–5).

John wraps up his book, and indeed the Bible itself, with a cry of longing and eager expectation: "Come, Lord Jesus!" (22:20).

Acknowledgments

NO WRITER IS AN ISLAND. AS EVERY SELF-AWARE AUTHOR KNOWS, a book does not happen without the help of lots of other people—assistance provided sometimes on purpose, other times by accident. That is certainly true in this case.

Fifth-grade Sunday school students. God's Story in 66 Verses began as a daydream while I was trying to figure out how to present the Bible to fifth-graders during summer Sunday school a few years ago. Fifth-graders are smart and aren't easily taken in by shoddy teaching. In my limited experience, they're open spiritually but must be *engaged*. I wondered if there was a simpler, more powerful way to summarize what each book of the Bible is about, and what the Bible as a whole is about. It occurred to me that certain verses in certain books in both Testaments describe the essentials. I wondered if it would be possible to compile a list with a verse for each Bible book. So I did, and this book was off and running. Thanks, fifth-graders, for refusing to accept the same ole, same ole, and for forcing me to be creative.

John Wilson. At a delicate time, my friend and colleague John Wilson, who is the editor of *Books & Culture*, introduced me to Joel Miller, a top-notch editor at Thomas Nelson. Joel quickly grasped the excitement of my idea, advocated for it at a first-rate publishing house, and offered me a contract. Only God knows if this volume would have seen the light of day without John . . . and Joel. (This is not the first time I have benefited professionally through my friendship with John, and I am very pleased to express my gratitude publicly.)

The ESV Study Bible, Mark Dever, and Walter Elwell. As I began writing this book, it quickly became apparent that my knowledge of the Bible could only take me so far. So I engaged the services of two experienced guides: Crossway's *ESV Study Bible* and Capitol Hill Baptist Church's Mark Dever. The former helped me formulate outlines of Bible books and provided exegetical, theological, and technical answers to my many questions, from a broadly Reformed perspective. The *ESV Study Bible* is like having a team of Bible scholars on your desk (but it's a lot less crowded). Dever's work often gave me the arc of a Bible book and plenty of pastoral applications, for Bible knowledge is meant to be lived. Walter Elwell, meanwhile, assisted my exploration of the massive book of Psalms. Without his published help, I might be wandering among its verses still. Thanks to you all!

Thomas Nelson. Thanks for the expert help from the rest of the team at Thomas Nelson, particularly Janene MacIvor and Kristen Parrish. Good publishing houses add the little things that an author forgets. They can turn a good book into a great one. May it be so with *God's Story in 66 Verses*. As always, any mistakes are my own fault.

Finally, my gratitude, as always, goes to Christine, my faithful, insightful, and encouraging wife (and dearest friend). Without you, Sweetheart, I wouldn't be in a position to tell God's story—or anyone else's. Aside from God and by his grace, you're the best thing that ever happened to me.

S.G.

Appendix

The Sixty-Six Verses

OLD TESTAMENT

1. Genesis 15:6

He believed the LORD, and he counted it to him as righteousness.

2. Exodus 19:5

If you will indeed obey my voice and keep my covenant, you shall be my treasured possession among all peoples, for all the earth is mine.

3. Leviticus 11:45

I am the LORD who brought you up out of the land of Egypt to be your God. You shall therefore be holy, for I am holy.

4. Numbers 14:9

Only do not rebel against the LORD. And do not fear the people of the land, for they are bread for us. Their protection is removed from them, and the LORD is with us; do not fear them.

5. Deuteronomy 5:29

Oh that they had such a heart as this always, to fear me and to keep all my commandments, that it might go well with them and with their descendants forever!

6. Joshua 1:6

Be strong and courageous, for you shall cause this people to inherit the land that I swore to their fathers to give them.

7. Judges 8:34

The people of Israel did not remember the LORD their God, who had delivered them from the hand of all their enemies on every side.

8. Ruth 1:16

Ruth said, "Do not urge me to leave you or to return from following you. For where you go I will go, and where you lodge I will lodge. Your people shall be my people, and your God my God."

9. 1 Samuel 2:35

I will raise up for myself a faithful priest, who shall do according to what is in my heart and in my mind. And I will build him a sure house, and he shall go in and out before my anointed forever.

10. 2 Samuel 7:16

Your house and your kingdom shall be made sure forever before me. Your throne shall be established forever.

11. 1 Kings 11:11

The LORD said to Solomon, "Since this has been your practice and you have not kept my covenant and my statutes that I have commanded you, I will surely tear the kingdom from you and will give it to your servant."

12. 2 Kings 17:13

Yet the LORD warned Israel and Judah by every prophet and every seer, saying, "Turn from your evil ways and keep my commandments and my statutes, in accordance with all the Law that I commanded your fathers, and that I sent to you by my servants the prophets."

13. 1 Chronicles 29:18

O LORD, the God of Abraham, Isaac, and Israel, our fathers, keep forever such purposes and thoughts in the hearts of your people, and direct their hearts toward you.

14. 2 Chronicles 7:14

If my people who are called by my name humble themselves, and pray and seek my face and turn from their wicked ways, then I will hear from heaven and will forgive their sin and heal their land.

15. Ezra 9:14

Shall we break your commandments again and intermarry with the peoples who practice these abominations? Would you not be angry with us until you consumed us, so that there should be no remnant, nor any to escape?

16. Nehemiah 1:11

"O Lord, let your ear be attentive to the prayer of your servant, and to the prayer of your servants who delight to fear your name, and give success to your servant today, and grant him mercy in the sight of this man."

Now I was cupbearer to the king.

17. Esther 4:14

If you keep silent at this time, relief and deliverance will rise for the Jews from another place, but you and your father's house will perish. And who knows whether you have not come to the kingdom for such a time as this?

18. Job 42:6

I despise myself,
  and repent in dust and ashes.

19. Psalm 16:11

You make known to me the path of life;
  in your presence there is fullness of joy;
  at your right hand are pleasures forevermore.

20. Proverbs 1:7

The fear of the LORD is the beginning of knowledge;
  fools despise wisdom and instruction.

21. Ecclesiastes 1:3

What does man gain by all the toil
  at which he toils under the sun?

22. Song of Songs 6:3

I am my beloved's and my beloved is mine;
  he grazes among the lilies.

23. Isaiah 40:9

Go on up to a high mountain,
  O Zion, herald of good news;

lift up your voice with strength,
  O Jerusalem, herald of good news;
    lift it up, fear not;
say to the cities of Judah,
  "Behold your God!"

24. Jeremiah 31:33

This is the covenant that I will make with the house of Israel after those days, declares the LORD: I will put my law within them, and I will write it on their hearts. And I will be their God, and they shall be my people.

25. Lamentations 3:22

The steadfast love of the LORD never ceases;
  his mercies never come to an end.

26. Ezekiel 36:22

Say to the house of Israel, Thus says the Lord GOD: It is not for your sake, O house of Israel, that I am about to act, but for the sake of my holy name, which you have profaned among the nations to which you came.

27. Daniel 6:26

I make a decree, that in all my royal dominion people are to tremble and fear before the God of Daniel,

  for he is the living God,
    enduring forever;
  his kingdom shall never be destroyed,
    and his dominion shall be to the end.

28. Hosea 6:4

What shall I do with you, O Ephraim?
  What shall I do with you, O Judah?
Your love is like a morning cloud,
  like the dew that goes early away.

29. Joel 2:28

It shall come to pass afterward,
  that I will pour out my Spirit on all flesh;
your sons and your daughters shall prophesy,
  your old men shall dream dreams,
  and your young men shall see visions.

30. Amos 5:24

Let justice roll down like waters,
  and righteousness like an ever-flowing stream.

31. Obadiah 4

Though you soar aloft like the eagle,
  though your nest is set among the stars,
  from there I will bring you down,
declares the LORD.

32. Jonah 4:2

He prayed to the LORD and said, "O LORD, is not this what I said when I was yet in my country? That is why I made haste to flee to Tarshish; for I knew that you are a gracious God and merciful, slow to anger and abounding in steadfast love, and relenting from disaster."

33. Micah 6:8

He has told you, O man, what is good;
  and what does the LORD require of you
but to do justice, and to love kindness,
  and to walk humbly with your God?

34. Nahum 1:3

The LORD is slow to anger and great in power,
  and the LORD will by no means clear the guilty.
His way is in whirlwind and storm,
  and the clouds are the dust of his feet.

35. Habakkuk 3:16

I hear, and my body trembles;
  my lips quiver at the sound;
rottenness enters into my bones;
  my legs tremble beneath me.
Yet I will quietly wait for the day of trouble
  to come upon people who invade us.

36. Zephaniah 3:7

I said, "Surely you will fear me;
  you will accept correction.
Then your dwelling would not be cut off
  according to all that I have appointed against you."
But all the more they were eager
  to make all their deeds corrupt.

37. Haggai 1:4

Is it a time for you yourselves to dwell in your paneled houses,
while this house lies in ruins?

38. Zechariah 8:23

Thus says the LORD of hosts: In those days ten men from the nations of every tongue shall take hold of the robe of a Jew, saying, "Let us go with you, for we have heard that God is with you."

39. Malachi 1:11

From the rising of the sun to its setting my name will be great among the nations, and in every place incense will be offered to my name, and a pure offering. For my name will be great among the nations, says the LORD of hosts.

NEW TESTAMENT

40. Matthew 16:15

He said to them, "But who do you say that I am?"

41. Mark 10:45

Even the Son of Man came not to be served but to serve, and to give his life as a ransom for many.

42. Luke 4:18

The Spirit of the Lord is upon me,
  because he has anointed me
  to proclaim good news to the poor.
He has sent me to proclaim liberty to the captives
  and recovering of sight to the blind,
  to set at liberty those who are oppressed.

43. John 1:14

The Word became flesh and dwelt among us, and we have seen his glory, glory as of the only Son from the Father, full of grace and truth.

44. Acts 1:8

You will receive power when the Holy Spirit has come upon you, and you will be my witnesses in Jerusalem and in all Judea and Samaria, and to the end of the earth.

45. Romans 1:16

I am not ashamed of the gospel, for it is the power of God for salvation to everyone who believes, to the Jew first and also to the Greek.

46. 1 Corinthians 12:13

In one Spirit we were all baptized into one body—Jews or Greeks, slaves or free—and all were made to drink of one Spirit.

47. 2 Corinthians 4:7

We have this treasure in jars of clay, to show that the surpassing power belongs to God and not to us.

48. Galatians 2:16

We know that a person is not justified by works of the law but through faith in Jesus Christ, so we also have believed in Christ Jesus, in order to be justified by faith in Christ and not by works of the law, because by works of the law no one will be justified.

49. Ephesians 2:8

By grace you have been saved through faith. And this is not your own doing; it is the gift of God.

50. Philippians 4:4

Rejoice in the Lord always; again I will say, rejoice.

51. Colossians 1:16

By him all things were created, in heaven and on earth, visible and invisible, whether thrones or dominions or rulers or authorities—all things were created through him and for him.

52. 1 Thessalonians 5:2

You yourselves are fully aware that the day of the Lord will come like a thief in the night.

53. 2 Thessalonians 2:2

Not to be quickly shaken in mind or alarmed, either by a spirit or a spoken word, or a letter seeming to be from us, to the effect that the day of the Lord has come.

54. 1 Timothy 3:15

If I delay, you may know how one ought to behave in the household of God, which is the church of the living God, a pillar and buttress of the truth.

55. 2 Timothy 1:8

Do not be ashamed of the testimony about our Lord, nor of me his prisoner, but share in suffering for the gospel by the power of God.

56. Titus 3:8

The saying is trustworthy, and I want you to insist on these things, so that those who have believed in God may be careful to devote themselves to good works. These things are excellent and profitable for people.

57. Philemon 10

I appeal to you for my child, Onesimus, whose father I became in my imprisonment.

58. Hebrews 4:14

Since then we have a great high priest who has passed through the heavens, Jesus, the Son of God, let us hold fast our confession.

59. James 1:22

Be doers of the word, and not hearers only, deceiving yourselves.

60. 1 Peter 4:13

Rejoice insofar as you share Christ's sufferings, that you may also rejoice and be glad when his glory is revealed.

61. 2 Peter 3:2

You should remember the predictions of the holy prophets and the commandment of the Lord and Savior through your apostles.

62. 1 John 1:3

That which we have seen and heard we proclaim also to you, so that you too may have fellowship with us; and indeed our fellowship is with the Father and with his Son Jesus Christ.

63. 2 John 6

This is love, that we walk according to his commandments; this is the commandment, just as you have heard from the beginning, so that you should walk in it.

64. 3 John 8

We ought to support people like these, that we may be fellow workers for the truth.

65. Jude 3

Beloved, although I was very eager to write to you about our common salvation, I found it necessary to write appealing to you to contend for the faith that was once for all delivered to the saints.

66. Revelation 1:19

Write therefore the things that you have seen, those that are and those that are to take place after this.

Selected Bibliography

Bartholomew, Craig G. *Ecclesiastes.* Grand Rapids: Baker Academic, 2009.

Bartholomew, Craig G., and Ryan P. O'Dowd. *Old Testament Wisdom Literature: A Theological Introduction.* Downers Grove: IVP Academic, 2001.

Bright, John. *A History of Israel.* 3rd ed. Philadelphia: Westminster Press, 1981.

Clinton, Rabbi Boruch. "Psalms (Tehilim)." Torah.org, http://www.torah.org/learning/basics/primer/torah/psalms.html#.

Dever, Mark. *The Message of the New Testament: Promises Kept.* Wheaton: Crossway, 2005.

———. *The Message of the Old Testament: Promises Made.* Wheaton: Crossway, 2006.

Elwell, Walter A., ed. *Baker Encyclopedia of the Bible.* Grand Rapids: Baker Book House, 1988.

———, ed. *Evangelical Commentary on the Bible.* Grand Rapids: Baker Book House, 1989.

Finegan, Jack. *Light from the Ancient Past: The Archeological Background of the Hebrew-Christian Religion.* Princeton: Princeton University Press, 1946.

Grant, Jr., James H. *1 and 2 Thessalonians: The Hope of Salvation.* Wheaton: Crossway, 2011.

Guthrie, Stan. *A Concise Guide to Bible Prophecy: 60 Predictions Everyone Should Know.* Grand Rapids: Baker Books, 2013.

Lawrence, Paul. *The IVP Atlas of Bible History.* Downers Grove: InterVarsity Press, 2006.

Longman III, Tremper, ed. *The Baker Illustrated Bible Dictionary.* Grand Rapids: Baker Books, 2013.

McDowell, Josh. *Evidence That Demands a Verdict.* San Bernardino: Here's Life Publishers, 1979.

Mounce, William D. *ESV Comprehensive Concordance of the Bible.* Wheaton: Crossway, 2012.

Piper, John. *A Sweet and Bitter Providence: Sex, Race, and the Sovereignty of God.* Wheaton: Crossway, 2010.

Taylor, Justin, ed. *ESV Study Bible*. Wheaton: Crossway, 2007.

Walton, John H. *Chronological and Background Charts of the Old Testament*. Grand Rapids: Zondervan, 1978.

———, ed. *The Minor Prophets, Job, Psalms, Proverbs, Ecclesiastes, Song of Songs*. Vol. 5. Zondervan Illustrated Bible Backgrounds Commentary. Grand Rapids: Zondervan, 2009.

Notes

3. Leviticus 11:45

1. These descriptions outlining Leviticus are borrowed generally from Justin Taylor, ed., *ESV Study Bible* (Wheaton: Crossway, 2007), using various notes on Leviticus. All references to Taylor in these notes are from this study Bible.
2. From the Westminster Shorter Catechism, answer to Question 1: "Man's chief end is to glorify God, and to enjoy him forever," http://www.reformed.org/documents/WSC.html.

5. Deuteronomy 5:29

1. Taylor, Deuteronomy, "History of Salvation Summary," 328.

6. Joshua 1:6

1. For a similar approach, see Taylor, Joshua, "Outline," 393.

8. Ruth 1:16

1. John Piper, *A Sweet and Bitter Providence: Sex, Race, and the Sovereignty of God* (Wheaton: Crossway, 2010), 12–13.
2. Judd H. Burton, "Chemosh—Lord of the Moabites," About.com, http://ancienthistory.about.com/od/cgodsandgoddesses/a/chemosh.htm.

12. 2 Kings 17:13

1. Mark Dever, *The Message of the Old Testament: Promises Made* (Wheaton: Crossway, 2006), 318.
2. Taylor, 2 Kings, note on 2:14, 648.

13. 1 Chronicles 29:18
   1. Taylor, 1–2 Chronicles, "Author and Title," 697.
   2. Ibid., "Purpose, Occasion, and Background," 697–98.

14. 2 Chronicles 7:14
   1. Taylor, 2 Chronicles, note on 7:14, 752.

15. Ezra 9:14
   1. Dever, *Old Testament*, 389.

16. Nehemiah 1:11
   1. See, for example, Paul Lawrence, *The IVP Atlas of Bible History* (Downers Grove: InterVarsity Press, 2006), 116.

17. Esther 4:14
   1. Taylor, Esther, "Author and Title," 849.
   2 Ibid., note on 3:1, 856.

19. Psalm 16:11
   1. Dever, *Old Testament*, 483.
   2. Walter Elwell, 2:1797–98.
   3. Ibid., 2:1798–1800.

20: Proverbs 1:7
   1. Dever, *Old Testament*, 511.

21. Ecclesiastes 1:3
   1. Dever, *Old Testament*, 528, emphasis in original.
   2. Craig G. Bartholomew, *Ecclesiastes* (Grand Rapids: Baker Academic, 2009), 106.

22. Song of Songs 6:3
   1. Taylor, Song of Songs, "Introduction to Song of Solomon," 1211–15.

23. Isaiah 40:9
   1. Esther and, according to some scholars, Song of Songs (giving a variant reading of Song 8:6).

24. Jeremiah 31:33
   1. Taylor, Jeremiah, "Author and Title," 1364.
   2. Ibid., 1364.

25. Lamentations 3:22

1. Taylor, Lamentations, "Literary Features," 1476.

26. Ezekiel 36:22

1. Taylor, Ezekiel, "Date," 1495.
2. Ibid., note on 40:1–48:35, 1564.

27. Daniel 6:26

1. Taylor, Daniel, note on 5:30–31, 1596–97.

29. Joel 2:28

1. Taylor, Joel, note on 1:15, 1647.
2. Ibid., note on 2:28–29, 1651.

31. Obadiah 4

1. Elwell, 1:656.
2. Taylor, Obadiah, note on vv. 2–4, 1680.
3. Josh McDowell, *Evidence That Demands a Verdict* (San Bernardino: Here's Life Publishers, 1979), 290.
4. John H. Walton, *The Minor Prophets, Job, Psalms, Proverbs, Ecclesiastes, Song of Songs, vol. 5, Zondervan Illustrated Bible Backgrounds Commentary* (Grand Rapids: Zondervan, 2009), 93.

34. Nahum 1:3

1. Stan Guthrie, *A Concise Guide to Bible Prophecy: 60 Predictions Everyone Should Know* (Grand Rapids: Baker Books, 2013), 51–52.

38. Zechariah 8:23

1. Taylor, Zechariah, "Zechariah's Visions," 1756.

41. Mark 10:45

1. Mark Dever, *The Message of the New Testament: Promises Kept* (Wheaton: Crossway, 2005), 61.
2. For an example of a similar take on Jesus' ministry, see Taylor, Mark, "Outline," 1891–92.

43. John 1:14

1. Taylor, John, "Key Themes," 2016.

44. Acts 1:8
1. Taylor, Acts, note on 18:23–21:16, 2124.

46. 1 Corinthians 12:13
1. As we have seen, Israel suffered from the same problem.

47. 2 Corinthians 4:7
1. Taylor, 2 Corinthians, "Date," "Purpose, Occasion, and Background," 2219–20.

52. 1 Thessalonians 5:2
1. Taylor, 1 Thessalonians, "The Second Coming in 1 Thessalonians," 2306.
2. See Isaiah 13:6; Joel 1:15; Amos 5:18.

53. 2 Thessalonians 2:2
1. Tremper Longman III, ed., *The Baker Illustrated Bible Dictionary* (Grand Rapids: Baker Books, 2013), 407.
2. Ibid.
3. Ibid., 408.
4. 1 Thessalonians 5:2; see chapter 52.
5. Taylor, Matthew, note on 24:15, 18:73.

54. 1 Timothy 3:15
1. See chapter 49 on Ephesians.

56. Titus 3:8
1. Longman, *Baker Illustrated Bible Dictionary*, 1640.
2. Taylor, Titus, note on 1:12, 2349.

57. Philemon 10
1. Dever, *New Testament*, 399.

58. Hebrews 4:14
1. Eusebius, *Ecclesiastical History* 6.25.14; quoted in Taylor, Hebrews, "Author, Audience, and Title," 2357.

59. James 1:22

1. Elwell, 2:1089–90.
2. Longman, *Baker Illustrated Bible Dictionary*, 890, referencing Eusebius, *Ecclesiastical History* 2.23.4–7.
3. Ibid., referencing Eusebius, *Ecclesiastical History* 2.23.16–18.

61. 2 Peter 3:2

1. See discussion in chapter 60.

62. 1 John 1:3

1. See chapter 43.
2. Longman, *Baker Illustrated Bible Dictionary*, 581.

63. 2 John 6

1. Taylor, 2 John, "Recipients," 2439.

64. 3 John 8

1. See, for example, Elwell 1:828, and Longman, *Baker Illustrated Bible Dictionary*, 627.
2. See 2 John 4.

65. Jude 3

1. See chapter 59.
2. It would be hard to find a clearer biblical reference to the fact that the Son of God, who was given the name Jesus in the New Testament, is the same God as the Yahweh of the Old Testament.
3. Matthew 25:31–46.
4. Matthew 12:36–37.

66. Revelation 1:19

1. See the author's book, *A Concise Guide to Bible Prophecy: 60 Predictions Everyone Should Know* (Grand Rapids: Baker Books, 2013).
2. Taylor, Revelation, "Structure and Outline," 2461–62.
3. Ibid, "Christ's Edict-letters to His Seven Churches," 2465.
4. John 1:29.
5. Taylor, Revelation, note on 8:6–11:18, 2475.
6. See, for example, Isaiah 61:1–2.

About the Author

STAN GUTHRIE, A *CHRISTIANITY TODAY* EDITOR AT LARGE, IS AUTHOR of *A Concise Guide to Bible Prophecy*, *All That Jesus Asks*, and *Missions in the Third Millennium*. He is also coauthor (with Jerry Root) of *The Sacrament of Evangelism*. Stan's work has been translated into Indonesian, Portuguese, and other languages. Stan writes regular opinion pieces for *BreakPoint.org* and *ChristianHeadlines.com*.

Stan, an inspirational speaker and teacher, is also host of the *Books & Culture* podcast and is a frequent radio commentator on current events and the evangelical scene. A book editor and literary agent, he has a master's in intercultural studies and a certificate in biblical studies from Columbia International University, as well as a bachelor's in journalism from the University of Florida.

Stan is happily (and gratefully) married to Christine. They have three children.

Printed in the USA
CPSIA information can be obtained
at www.ICGtesting.com
CBHW010633210124
3503CB00004B/25

9 781400 206421